MONARCH NOTES

Edith Wharton's
ETHAN FROME

A CRITICAL COMMENTARY

CHARLES LEAVITT

ASSOCIATE PROFESSOR OF ENGLISH
MONTCLAIR STATE COLLEGE

MONARCH PRESS

CONTENTS

INTRODUCTION

BRIEF ACCOUNT OF EDITH WHARTON'S LIFE: EARLY LIFE. Mrs. Wharton was born Edith Newbold Jones on January 24, 1862, in her parents' mansion on West Twenty-Third Street in New York City. Her mother, Lucretia Stevens Rhinelander, connected with wealthy Dutch landowners and merchants of the early nineteenth century, was the granddaughter of an outstanding American Revolutionary War patriot, General Ebenezer Stevens. After the war, General Stevens became a very successful East-India merchant. Edith Wharton's father, a man of considerable private, inherited wealth, did not follow a career in business. Rather, he lived a life of leisure, punctuated by his hobbies of sea-fishing, boat-racing, and wild-fowl shooting (typical activities for men of wealth of his day). During her first few years, Edith Wharton's family alternated between New York City in the winter and Newport, Rhode Island, in the summer. (Newport was a very fashionable place where New York City families of wealth might enjoy ocean breezes and participate in a round of tea and dinner parties, the leaving of calling cards, and constant preparations for entertaining or being entertained.)

When she was four years old, her parents took her on a tour of Europe, concentrating on Italy and France. She became as familiar with Rome and Paris as any American child is familiar with his home town. During these early years, the small, red-haired Edith played a favorite game. Not yet able to read, she carried around with her a large volume of Washington Irving's stories of old Spain, *The Alhambra*. Holding the book carefully (sometimes upside down), she proceeded to turn the pages and to read aloud "make up" stories as she went along. Whereas most children of her age would be told the familiar old folk and fairy tales of Andersen, Perrault, and the Brothers Grimm, she listened with great delight to tales of the "domestic dramas" of the great Greek and Roman gods of mythology. (Some of the fictional characters in her literary works do resemble gods in distress, followed by some unhappy curse or fate.) One can picture young Edith Wharton in Paris, as she arrives from her dancing-lesson and goes immediately

5

to her grandmother, seated in a comfortable armchair. Through an ear-trumpet at her grandmother's ear, the seven-year-old Edith would shout Tennyson's *Idylls of the King,* much to the old woman's delight. Edith's father's constant reading of travel books was of interest to the child, who was to travel through Europe and America much of her own lifetime. The Wharton family in Paris was saddened by the beginning of the Franco-Prussian War and also by the near-fatal attack of typhoid fever which Edith suffered. The young child rapidly learned to read, speak, and write German, French, and Italian, as a result of the efforts of governesses and the extended family tours of France and Italy.

RETURN TO AMERICA AND BACKGROUND READING. Returning to America after an absence of six years in picturesque Europe, the ten-year-old Edith viewed New York City with mixed feelings. She missed the glamor of Europe; she was distressed with the busy commercial air of much of her home city; she was delighted to join her relatives and friends on a rambling family estate (Pencraig) at Newport. Here she continued her study of modern languages and good manners. She was fascinated by archery club meetings; she pictured in her mind the archery players ("young gods and goddesses") as characters in unwritten works of fiction. She read much of the prose of Mark Twain, Bret Harte, and Lewis Carroll, as well as the nonsense poetry of Edward Lear. The proper command of good speech was impressed upon the child by her parents. Returning from the open countryside of Newport to the cramped city of New York, Edith began to read regularly in her father's library of standard classics. She read many books, including the following: the "principal historians," such as the Roman Plutarch and the English Macaulay; the foremost writers of diaries and letters, such as the English Pepys and Evelyn, and the French Madame de Sévigné; the English poets, such as Milton, Burns and Byron, as well as Scott, Wordsworth, Coleridge, Shelley, and Elizabeth Barrett Browning; the English Sir Walter Scott and the American Washington Irving. With these writers as her models and inspiration, young Edith Wharton began to cover huge sheets of wrapping paper with her own prose and verse.

MARRIAGE. Edith's family and the families of most of her friends were not "in business": they lived on their incomes (sometimes investments), living leisurely lives of "dining out" or "dinner-giving," with much emphasis on good cooking and sparkling conversation. Once in awhile, they attended the theatre; the opera, seldom. When she was seventeen, Edith's parents decided the time had arrived for her "coming-out" (a series of social activities indicating to the world that she was adult enough to be invited to social entertainments without her parents as chaperones). Soon, she joined her father and mother for another trip to Europe—this time for her father's health. He died in France, when Edith was nineteen years old, and the grief-stricken mother and daughter returned to New York City. There they moved into a newly purchased house on West Twenty-fifth Street. For several years Edith enjoyed the social life of an average young woman of her wealth and social background; then her girlhood came to an end in 1885 with her marriage to Edward Wharton of Boston. Thirteen years her senior, her husband was a banker from Boston. (His father's family had originally come from Virginia.) Although Mr. Wharton did not share his wife's literary tastes, he did, however, enjoy some of her interests, such as animals, outdoor life, and (especially) travel. For a time the couple lived in a cottage on the Pencraig estate in Newport. Each February they began a tour of Europe extending over four months. Edith prepared herself for these annual trips by wide reading, especially of books on architecture. One happy period of four months (in 1888) was spent with friends on a rented yacht, touring the waters of the Mediterranean and the Aegean Seas. One holiday was spent on an excursion through the hills of northern Italy, which were later to form the background of Mrs. Wharton's first novel, *The Valley of Decision* (1902), a historical romance of eighteenth-century Italy. The Whartons bought a house at Newport called "Land's End." There, Mrs. Wharton carried out some of her own original ideas about interior decoration—a project which later blossomed out into a book written in collaboration with the decorator-architect, Ogden Codman. This book, *The Decoration of Houses* (1897), was based upon Mrs. Wharton's own experimental ideas concerning the decoration of houses, and featured the then new ideas of emphasis on simplicity of detail, right proportion, balance of door and window-spacing, and unconfused lines.

FIRST PUBLICATIONS AND LITERARY FRIENDS. Mrs. Wharton's first publications were poems, accepted and published by the editor of *Scribner's Magazine,* who also helped make arrangements to bring out in print *The Decoration of Houses.* With the publication in *Scribner's Magazine* of her first short story, "Mrs. Manstey's View," she began her long publishing career in fiction. When, to her delighted surprise, a publisher decided to bring forth a collected group of her short stories under the title *The Greater Inclination* (1899), she suddenly began to have a "real personality" of her own: she was no longer just one of the idle, cultured rich; she was an acknowledged individual, all on her own, and in print. She need not care that in Boston (her husband's home town) she was considered to have more fashion than intelligence, whereas in New York (her home area) some thought her to possess more intelligence than fashion. Putting this intelligence to work, Mrs. Wharton went to Rome in the winter of 1903, where she began a serious study of Italian villas. The result of this study was a work entitled *Italian Villas and Their Gardens* (1904), featuring watercolors by the well-known American painter and illustrator, Maxfield Parrish. Although Europe held much interest for Edith, she had, at least, found a spot in America where she could realize her greatest happiness and contentment. The place was near Lenox, in the Berkshire hills of western Massachusetts. After selling the Newport house, the Whartons built a large, rambling country house, which they called "The Mount." For over ten years (for six or seven months a year), she found ample room and time for gardening, writing, and making excursions throughout the neighboring hills. (*Ethan Frome* was inspired by the people and natural setting she observed near Lenox.) The early part of each winter she spent in New York City. There, as well as in Lenox, she met and talked with some of her artistic friends, such as William Dean Howells and Henry James (the novelists), Charles Eliot Norton (the famous American educator, editor and author), and Clyde Fitch (the popular American playwright). During frequent trips abroad, she was friendly with Thomas Hardy, Mrs. Humphry Ward, and George Meredith (literary artists), as well as the renowned portrait-artist, John Singer Sargent. After Mr. Wharton's health began to fail, the couple traveled often in France, Spain, Italy, Germany, Sicily, and northern Africa, to avoid the coldness of the New York winters.

From 1907, Mrs. Wharton spent most of her time near Paris, where she entertained fashionable and literary society and a few visiting Americans (such as Theodore Roosevelt, during his 1909-1910 world tour). When she traveled to London, she made a special point of seeing as much as possible Henry James, who had taken up residence there. Life in Paris flowed quietly along for Edith Wharton, as she enjoyed stimulating conversations with both intellectual and fashionable Parisians, such as Jacques-Emile Blanche (the famous French painter and literary artist) and Madame de Fitz-James and the guests in her salon (a drawing room used as a gathering place of noted persons, usually under the patronage of some distinguished woman). Enjoying numerous complimentary comments about her novel *The House of Mirth* (1905), Mrs. Wharton produced several volumes of short stories. Then she began composing and writing, with the "greatest joy" and the "fullest ease," *Ethan Frome*. (Mrs. Wharton began the composition of *Ethan Frome* in Paris *in French,* to have practice in keeping up-to-date with French idioms.) Along about this time, she participated in some very pleasurable experiences. She continued to socialize with her literary idol, Henry James. She thrilled to the dancing of the superb ballerina, Isadora Duncan, at the Paris Opera. She was inspired by the Imperial ballet from St. Petersburg, under the direction of Diaghilev, the famed Russian ballet producer. She experienced a great sense of excitement over Marcel Proust's first volume of *Remembrance of Things Past*. These new joys were somewhat dimmed by sad events. Each summer had seen the return of the Whartons to their glorious summer place, "The Mount," in Lenox, Massachusetts. Over a period of years, Mr. Wharton's health gradually began to fail due to neurasthenia (a condition marked by general physical weakness, depression and bodily disturbances). The summer place was sold, for Mrs. Wharton was not able to care for it all alone.

FRANCE AND THE WAR EFFORT. Back in France, during the early days of World War I, Mrs. Wharton saw the suffering of the sick and the homeless. Almost immediately, she began to do Red Cross work; she even provided a place for women who could sew clothing for the needy. To excite American interest in the plight of the French, she made six trips to the battle lines and then wrote an account of the hospital needs of the wounded. A woman with a tender heart for the sufferings of others, Mrs. Wharton and her many helpers cared for thousands of war refugees and several large groups of the young and the aged, as well as maintaining four sanatoriums for women and children who were victims of tuberculosis. Her heroic war efforts were recognized by France in 1915 when she was awarded the Cross of the Legion of Honor. Belgium, in 1916, made her Chevalier (knight) of the Order of Leopold. To help obtain money for war relief work, Mrs. Wharton put together *The Book of the Homeless*, made up of original poems, articles, and drawings donated by some of the leading members of the literary and artistic world in Europe and America. In addition to all of her other demanding duties at the time, Mrs. Wharton translated into English the great majority of the Italian and French contributions to the book. Her great understanding and sympathy for France and the French people are seen in the works written during the years centering around World War I: *Fighting France* (1915); *The Marne* (1918); and *French Ways and Their Meaning* (1919).

LAST DAYS. When World War I was over, Edith Wharton busied herself with the writing of what turned out to be one of her greatest novels, *The Age of Innocence*. A picture of New York society of the 1870's, the book was published in 1920 and received the Pulitzer Prize for 1921. She alternated between her two homes in France—one near Paris and one in Provence. After a 1926 yacht trip in the Mediterranean Sea, she lived quietly in France for the remainder of her days. She wrote constantly, but her later work never achieved the sharp and sensitive flavor of her earlier, popular novels (such as *The House of Mirth, Ethan Frome, The Custom of the Country,* and *The Age of Innocence*). She died in St. Brice, France, August 11, 1937, and was buried at Versailles in the Protestant cemetery.

EDITH WHARTON'S SEPARATE WORKS LISTED CHRONOLOGICALLY

EARLY PERIOD

The Decoration of Houses (with Ogden Codman, Jr.), 1897
The Greater Inclination, 1899
The Touchstone, 1900
Crucial Instances, 1901
The Valley of Decision, 1902
Sanctuary, 1903
Italian Villas and Their Gardens, 1904
The Descent of Man and Other Stories, 1904
Italian Backgrounds, 1905

MIDDLE, MOST IMPORTANT PERIOD

The House of Mirth, 1905
Madame de Treymes, 1907
The Fruit of the Tree, 1907
A Motor-Flight Through France, 1908
The Hermit and the Wild Woman, and Other Stories, 1908
Artemis to Actaeon and Other Verse, 1909
Tales of Men and Ghosts, 1910.
Ethan Frome, 1911
The Reef, 1912
The Custom of the Country, 1913
Fighting France: From Dunkerque to Belfort, 1915
Xingu and Other Stories, 1916
Summer, 1917
The Marne, 1918
French Ways and Their Meaning, 1919
The Age of Innocence, 1920

LATER PERIOD

In Morocco, 1920
The Glimpses of the Moon, 1922
A Son at the Front, 1923
Old New York, 1924

The Mother's Recompense, 1925
The Writing of Fiction, 1925
Here and Beyond, 1926
Twelve Poems, 1926
Twilight Sleep, 1927
The Children, 1928
Hudson River Bracketed, 1929
Certain People, 1930
The Gods Arrive, 1932
Human Nature, 1933
A Backward Glance, 1934
The World Over, 1936
Ghosts, 1937
The Buccaneers, 1938

BRIEF SUMMARIES OF EDITH WHARTON'S LITERARY CONTRIBUTIONS

EARLY WORKS. Edith Wharton began writing fiction during her childhood, as she attempted to describe the manners of her own social set. Her first published work, however, was in the form of poetry—a sonnet entitled "Happiness," published in a magazine, *Scribner's,* in 1889. Two years later she followed this with a short story (also published in Scribner's), "Mrs. Manstey's View." Her first published book was not a work of fiction, for it was a joint effort (with Ogden Codman, Jr.) called *The Decoration of Houses* (1897). In 1899 she began her true literary career with a collection of short stories entitled *The Greater Inclination.*

LONG WORKS OF FICTION. Mrs. Wharton's long works of fiction (the novelette and the novel) are many. *The Touch-stone* (1900), written under the influence of Henry James, is concerned with a man's ethical decision centering about his sale of love letters sent him by a famous woman. He considers using the money he receives as the basis of financial security for his marriage. Her first long novel is *The Valley of Decision* (1902), a historical romance set in late eighteenth century Italy, featuring an aristocrat who is basically a liberal. The ironic twist at the end of this conventional work is that the hero, Otho, turns his back on his own previous liberal policies. He personally cannot accept the "improvements" he once fought for. In this work, the carefully pictured setting is more notable than the standard plot. *Sanctuary* (1903) explores a mother's fears for her son who has inherited some of his father's weaknesses of character. She guides him into an ethical choice not to cheat in an architectural contest, though he faces the possibility of losing the love of the girl he greatly admires. In *The House of Mirth* (1905), Lily Bart presents the tragic picture of a beautiful New York City girl who attempts to enter into a marriage of wealth and position. She gradually slides down the social ladder and finally ends up an unhappy suicide. (Numerous literary critics consider this novel one of Mrs. Wharton's finest works of fiction.) The 1907 novelette, *Madame de Treymes,* written in the style of Henry

13

James, contrasts different points of view toward marriage and divorce, love and honor, as seen by Americans and French. *The Fruit of the Tree* (1907) pictures the struggle of an American to better social and working conditions in a New England woolen-mill town. He is torn between his projected reforms and the two women in his life. A mercy-killing in the story adds a curious twist. *Ethan Frome* (1911) is a novelette concerning tragedy in the lives of three humble New England farm folks. Social conventions and poverty tie down a rebellious spirit. *The Reef* (1912), written in the manner of Henry James, shows an American diplomat in France involved in social and moral problems. While waiting to join his childhood sweetheart, George Darrow has a brief affair with a young woman, thus causing his true love affair to be wrecked upon a "reef." *The Custom of the Country* (1913) describes the antics of an American western heroine, Undine Spragg, who roams from fashionable New York to the social high spots of Europe as she conquers man after man. She represents the new aristocracy of money and idleness which Mrs. Wharton later describes so well in *The Age of Innocence*. Undine Spragg is one of Wharton's more interesting "heroines." *Summer* (1917), set in the hill country of western Massachusetts (the locale of *Ethan Frome*), pictures the bitter consequences inflicted upon an unhappy woman by poverty and desertion in love. *The Age of Innocence* (1920), winner of the 1921 Pulitzer Prize in fiction, considers the conflict in Victorian New York between the old aristocratic families ("clans") and the new social groups whose power and influence stem from industrial endeavors. Ellen Olenska, who returns from Europe and attempts to rebel against the traditional codes and prudishness of her American relatives, is one of Mrs. Wharton's most fascinating women characters. *The Glimpses of the Moon* (1922), shows the frustration involved when an American couple plan to "live off" rich friends in Europe. Their idea almost ends in their being separated from each other. In *A Son at the Front* (1923), the struggle is reviewed of an American painter living in Paris at the beginning of World War I, who finally gives his stepson to the army for France and the preservation of "beauty." *Old New York* (1924), a collection of four novelettes, is a series of fascinating pictures of mid-nineteenth-century New York life from the 1840's through the 1870's. "False Dawn" (the 1840's) describes the adventures of a young man touring in Europe, who does not buy "Old Masters" as he has been instructed by his wealthy father. Instead, he purchases a group of almost unknown Pre-Raphaelite paintings, which much later become very valuable. "The Old Maid" (the 1850's), once made into a splendid film starring Bette Davis, depicts the heartbreak involved when an unmarried woman allows her married sister to adopt her own child. "The Spark" (the 1860's) pictures a New York gentleman whose humdrum life has been made pleasant by his memories of a kind male hospital nurse who aided him during the Civil War when he was hospitalized in Washington; the friend turns out to have been Walt Whitman. "New Year's Day" (the 1870's) describes a woman's attempt to keep herself and her ill husband alive by becoming the mistress of another man. Later, after the death of her husband, her lover proposes marriage to her. She refuses, explaining her previous reasons for involvement with him. In *The Mother's Recompense* (1925), a mother returns after many years in Europe to find her grown-up daughter emotionally associated with a man she herself had once lived with; she does not reveal her past involvement with her daughter's fiancé, and she quietly goes back to Europe. *Twilight Sleep* (1927) pictures the New York society of the 1920's, the new aristocracy of power and money, introduced earlier in *The Age of Innocence*. Only two characters (a father and his daughter) regret the passing of the old, quiet, aristocratic first families. *The Children* (1928) explores the world of divorce which results in separated parents and unwanted children. A sixteen-year-old girl cares for seven children from broken homes. *Hudson River Bracketed* (1929) describes the attempts at revolt of a man against the pettiness, of small-town life in the Midwest. He comes to the East and finally becomes involved in a rather sordid love affair which could have been typical of his Midwestern home town. *The Gods Arrive* (1932), a sequel to *Hudson River Bracketed*, takes the main characters to Europe in their search for love. They end up believing that they will only find true happiness in fidelity to each other and marriage. Her unfinished novel, *The Buccaneers* (1938), pictures young American women in their effort to enter British society.

SHORT STORIES, CRITICISM, AND AUTOBIOGRAPHY. Mrs. Wharton's short stories were collected and published in the following volumes: *The Greater Inclination* (1899); *Crucial Instances* (1901); *The Descent of Man* (1904); *The Hermit and the Wild Woman* (1908); *Tales of Men and Ghosts* (1910); *Xingu and Other Stories* (1916); *Here and Beyond* (1926); *Certain People* (1930); *Human Nature* (1933); *The World Over* (1936); and *Ghosts* (1937). Of especial interest are *Tales of Men and Ghosts* (in which the different ghosts represent a variety of men's obsessions) and *Xingu and Other Stories* (where Mrs. Wharton's major literary themes are explored in small segments). Mrs. Wharton's three travel books reflect her international background: *Italian Villas and Their Gardens* (1904); *Italian Backgrounds* (1905); *A Motor-Flight Through France* (1908); *French Ways and Their Meaning* (1919); and *In Morocco* (1920). Mrs. Wharton published two books during World War I, illustrating her high respect for France and its part in the "Great War": *Fighting France: From Dunkerque to Belfort* (1915), a nonfictional account of her impression concerning the first years of the war; and *The Marne* (1918), a novel of only average impact and appeal. Both of these two books expressed her disapproval of the early American neutrality in World War I. Her statement of her artistic beliefs is in her own work of literary criticism, *The Writing of Fiction* (1925), in which she admits her artistic debt to Henry James, who was also concerned with "moral values," "classical unity," and "economy of means." She emphasizes that individual "characters" must react to the "situations" in which they find themselves. Her autobiography, *A Backward Glance* (1934), is her account of her childhood, comments on her early friends and travels, pictures of the society worlds of New York, Paris, and London, as well as the description of her helpful participation in World War I with refugees, and a summary of her friendship with Henry James.

SUMMARY. Mrs. Wharton's works have ranged over considerable literary ground. She has had published literary works in the following ten categories: a study of interior decoration; short stories; poetry; a historical romance; novels; novelettes; travel books; a book of war impressions; literary criticism; and autobiography. Although she has been highly commended for all of her published works, her greatest achievement is undoubtedly in the area of the novel, featuring such literary masterworks as *The House of Mirth, Ethan Frome,* and *The Age of Innocence.*

AN APPRECIATION OF *ETHAN FROME*

The consensus of critical appraisal of *Ethan Frome* holds that it is brilliant in form and design but lacking in feeling and depth; that its characters are polished but sterile: complete but unfelt; that its setting is elegantly staged rather than real-isically presented. This view appears to be accurate—if one uses the naturalistic novel and its offspring, the novel of in-terior consciousness, as the ideal and basis of comparison. But it is an inflexible insistence on this viewpoint that has made *Ethan Frome* a critical failure, rather than the particular lack of merit of the book itself. From another viewpoint, the stature of *Ethan Frome* is considerably larger, and its execu-tion in about all respects considerably more successful. This viewpoint can appreciate the value of a more classical de-sign: the formal tragedy.

FROM ATHENS TO STARKFIELD: It would be fatuous to say that *Ethan Frome* ranks in the hierarchy of worth with its ancient predecessors, the tragedies of the great Greek play-wrights, Aeschylus and Sophocles. But certainly it belongs in their line, and not the lines of Flaubert or Joyce, Edith Wharton's contemporary, and the basis of its intrinsic value and its long popular success lies in those same elements that have made those old plays live for some two thousand years. Like them, the novel presents the story of a unique person, larger than life, who is doomed by fate, and who finally com-mits the irrevocable act that brings the full weight of his destiny down upon him.

Like the characters of those plays, the characters in *Ethan Frome* are complex but formal embodiments of certain types, attitudes and ideas. Like the setting of a play, the town of Starkfield, its implacable winters and the unbending poverty of rural New England, is a carefully executed proscenium de-sign. Like the story of those plays, the final outcome is hinted at in the beginning, and only the process through which the hero's fate was made manifest are recreated. But although the old plays are still valued by our culture, we can hardly call them popular, while *Ethan Frome* has been very much a popular success in our time. This is due to the fact that *Ethan Frome* combines the power of the ancient story pattern with the charged meaning of an ancestral American scene, the New England town and country, and uses as its hero an ancestral American figure, the New England Puritan farmer to whom we can relate. Whether we like this figure or not, he is an intrinsic part of the American self-image, very much as an individual ancestor is recognized as part of the individual contemporary man. As such, his image has a certain power and importance for us, and by using it, *Ethan Frome* brings the meaningfulness of the old story two thousand years forward to the doorstep of the present.

THE REALITY IN TRAGEDY: But before we can appreciate the way that Edith Wharton used the ancient pattern to devise the story of Ethan Frome, we need to ask what it is in that pattern that gives it its vitality. Essentially, the answer lies in the fact that it is the story of every man as he sees himself. Although the society may consider some people fortunate and some abandoned by fortune, most people find much of their life difficult. Like Ethan Frome we find ourselves constrained by outer circumstance, and yet in retrospect, many of the serious difficulties of our lives seem to have been brought on by our own acts, and especially, through our attempts to overcome those circumstances. We can therefore identify with an individual who suffers from the circumstances of his life, and who fails in an attempt to overcome them. At the same time we can view the fate of the hero—and therefore of Ethan Frome—as a punishment, for invariably the tragic hero's grasp at freedom involves the violation of a basic ethic of his society. Thus, as we finish a truly tragic story, we feel for a moment as if there were a logic and a "right way" to life after all (whether or not we like that way), and for that moment, we feel as if there is a comforting logic to our own existence to counteract our sense of the unpredictability of life.

OF WORDS AND HEROES: But at least two more elements seem to be necessary before we take a formal tragedy to heart. One is that the character of the hero must be as unique as every individual secretly feels himself to be, as different from those about him as they seem like each other. The Greek playwrights accomplished this by making their heroes princes or kings. As we shall see, Edith Wharton creates Ethan as a unique person, but in a far more subtle way than did the Greek writers. And to his uniqueness, she adds an important element which makes it possible for the reader to identify strongly with her hero: the fact that he (like most readers) was capable of being and doing far more than his circumstances permitted.

The other element is beauty of language, and it is here that *Ethan Frome* is sadly lacking. It is not the *formality* of the narrative by which the book falls, for the Greek plays were formal enough even in their own time and yet stood high. It is rather that the language and phrasing are pedestrian, without that inner poetry for which the human ear most listens. It is as if in a work of written art, *how* we go is as important as *where* we are going. Unfortunately, even the colloquial New England language that Edith Wharton's characters use in the novel is stilted and flat. But the degree to which the novel stands despite this vital lack testifies to excellence with which the author used the structure of tragedy; to the brilliance of her setting and the construction of her characters; and to the logic and tightness of the action.

A CHORUS OF ONE: While Edith Wharton uses many of the elements of formal tragedy, she does not, of course, use its trappings. Instead of kings and palaces, she uses poor people and farm houses. Instead of having her characters speak in "elevated" tones, they use colloquial language. But she borrowed one formality of the old plays and transformed it to her purpose: the "chorus." In the Greek plays, the play always begins with a chorus, a group of bystanders who have no part in the action, but who set the scene, warn the audience of impending doom, and comment intermittently on the play. In *Ethan Frome*, this function is performed by a "chorus" of one—the engineer through whom we first see the town of Starkfield and meet Ethan Frome, and with whom we enter Ethan's grim household of today *before* the action starts. While he does not *comment* on the action as it proceeds, he does reflect this aspect of the chorus insofar as he appears again at the end of the story to tell us how everything turned out.

Since the story takes place in the past, and ends with the fatal act which leaves Ethan crippled, we need him to learn of the final twist of Ethan's fate and how he was "punished." If it were not for this "chorus," we would not know how the two apposite women in Ethan's life—his wife Zenobia, whom he hated, and her beautiful young cousin Mattie, who was the object of his "fatal passion"—had become virtually identical harpies. It is through his eyes that we see the accomplishments of fate in the novel: we see the cruel Zenobia humbled in her servitude to the crippled, whinning Mattie; we see Mattie's dancing feet forever stilled; but above all we learn the "lesson" of the story. It is the appalled description of the engineer that makes us realize that the terrible poverty of the scene ("Even for that part of the country the kitchen was a poor-looking place") and "the oppressive reality" of the two dreadful crones is, more than his own physical suffering, Ethan's punishment. More than that we have his conversation with Mrs. Hale, his landlady in Starkfield, which enables him to report that not only is this Ethan's punishment, but that Ethan *knows* it is. This is made clear when she says: "It's bad enough to see the two women sitting there—but *his* face, when he looks round that bare place, just kills me."

ECHOES FROM *THE INFERNO*: The reader's feeling that he is witness to a "damnation" is also underscored by the engineer's report of the final words of Mrs. Hale at the end of the book where she says that there is not much difference between the Fromes up at the farm and the Fromes down in the graveyard—" 'cept that down there they're all quiet, and the women have got to hold their tongues." The aspect of *eternal* punishment and damnation, however, is not derived from the Greeks: their "Hades" was just a dark place where the dead dwelt. The vision of a tortured damned is Christian in origin, and its conception was perfected by the fourteenth-century Italian poet, Dante, in his *Divine Comedy*.

To appreciate fully the depth which Mrs. Wharton has achieved in *Ethan Frome*, it is important to realize that it not only contains the elements of Greek tragedy but also echoes of this great work. In the first part of the *Divine Comedy*, "The Inferno," Dante descends through the nine circles of Hell. This

is the Hell we know: the hell of terror and desolations, where
the evil are tortured eternally for sins committed in life. There
we can find a possible model for the story of Ethan and Mattie
in two lovers, Paolo and Francesca, who are bound together
forever to be blown about ceaselessly by cold, turbulent winds.
They are in the second circle of Hell, where, Dante tells us,
"are condemned/The sinners of the flesh, who viley yield/
Their reason to their carnal appetite." Like Ethan and Mattie,
Paolo and Francesca were two innocents who "yielded to their
passion" and tried to commit suicide together. Both couples of
course succeeded, but in different ways.

A CHRISTIAN HELL: Thus, when the engineer sets the scene
for us, it is not in Greek but in the Christian terms, and grim-
mer still, in terms of Puritan Protestantism. The nature of the
scene in the present is introduced in the very name of Starkfield, but the author does not stop there. Bit by bit, she has
the engineer drop casual comments about what he sees about
him. When he notes the difference between the vitality of the
climate and the deadness of the community, we have our first
clue. When he says that Ethan seemed to be an "incarnation
of the mute melancholy landscape," that Ethan lives "in a
depth of moral isolation" and that his loneliness was not merely
the result of his personal plight but of "the profound accumu-
lation of many Starkfield winters"—we can be fairly certain of
where we are: in a hell on earth. As we approach Ethan's
house for the first time, the author uses two images that con-
firm the setting: the "starved apple trees writhing over a hill-
side" and the "black wraith of a deciduous creeper (that)
flapped from the porch." Mrs. Wharton uses the narrator to
add to her meaning when she has him say that, "in the distress
and oppression of the scene I did not know what to answer."

The author's skillful use of the weather as a device in *Ethan
Frome* can be seen most clearly if we note the contrast between the weather of Ethan Frome's *present* hell as it is described by the engineer, and the weather of the story itself.
The weather that the engineer and Ethan pass through as
Ethan drives him home, is a gale blowing over "a landscape
chaotically tossed." When they reach Ethan's home and decide
to give up for the night, it is because of the "bitter cold and
heavy going."

But the moment the narrator stops and the story begins, the weather is totally different: all is quiet in the "transparent" night. As Ethan waits by the church for the end of the dance so that he can take Mattie home, the night is "perfectly still, and the air so dry and pure that is gives little sensation of cold." The air remains like this throughout most of the story: the day that Zenobia (or Zeena) leaves to visit her sister overnight, the winter morning "is clear as crystal." The day that Mattie is to leave, the fields lie "like a silver shield under the sun." Only on the day between, the day Zeena returns and announces that Mattie must leave, is the weather bad; but even then it only rains: it is not the fierce, freezing blizzard of Hell.

TWO USES OF POVERTY: Edith Wharton uses one other element of the New England scene, both as an aspect of fate and as a confirmation of the depth to which Ethan falls. This is Ethan's poverty. Again we have a strong contrast between the poverty that the engineer describes for us and the poverty that drives the characters to their desperation. In the story itself, Ethan lives on the border of poverty. There is not enough money to pay his and Mattie's fare for an escape westward, and Mattie's own poverty makes her dependent upon the bounty of her cousin Zeena. Thus it is poverty-as-fate that makes it impossible for the lovers to rise above the circumstances which are to separate them, and it is poverty which drives them to their desperate attempt to commit suicide by driving their sleigh into the huge elm at the bottom of the hill. But the poverty that we see through the eyes of the engineer is of a different order. Here, poverty does not merely prevent escape from Starkfield, but grinds daily down upon the Frome house until its inhabitants are reduced to tattered shadows. We only need to refer to the adjectives the engineer uses to describe the awful scene in the epilogue to the novel. Zeena is bony, sallow, and slatternly; Mattie is slight, bloodless, shrivelled; the "meager furniture is of the roughest kind"; the dishes are coarse, cracked, and battered. When the engineer learns that for a dollar, the proud Ethan Frome would be willing to chauffeur him back and forth from the place where the narrator must catch his train each day, he expresses surprise. He knew Frome was poor, he says, but adds that he "had not supposed him to be in such want." The first kind of poverty is limiting; it is a familiar aspect of the human condition. The second kind destroys the body and spirit; it is the poverty of the damned.

THE CURSE IN POVERTY: Before we leave the aspects of fate and damnation, it will be useful to note how Edith Wharton uses the idea of the family curse as fate in *Ethan Frome*. Here we have precedents in both Greek and Protestant concepts. In many of the Greek stories, the hero is cursed from birth, or his family has been cursed before him. In the Greek story of Agamemnon, for instance, there is frequent reference to the curse on the house of Atreus, whereby we know that there is something in Agamemnon's life that dooms him no matter what he does. The Protestant idea is that the bad luck of a family or of an individual is visible evidence of God's disfavor. This concept was developed in Lutheranism, which held that God does not only judge a man in his after-life, but in his life on earth. Thus if a man and his family are wealthy and healthy they must be good; if they are poor and sick they must be bad. (Much of the American idea of the importance of success is derived from this antique idea.) Furthermore, the suffering of the children is justified in the Protestant view by the Biblical tenet that the sins of the father descend upon his children, "to the seventh generation of them that hate me."

Obviously, then, if Ethan Frome is crippled and poor; if his father had gone "soft in the brain" and had given away all his money; if his mother was "queer" and "weak as a baby"; and if his wife is constantly sick—then Ethan's father must have done something very bad, and Ethan's lot is God's punishment. We also see the intimation of a curse in Mattie's life, when we learn that her father died bankrupt after embezzling his relative's money. Here we know the father's sin and its consequences. We know that her mother died upon the disclosure of the facts, and that Mattie's "misfortune had, in a sense, indentured her" to the Fromes. We also know that Mattie's inability to earn her own living arises out of the well-to-do circumstances under which she was brought up. Thus the immediate circumstances of both their lives were created by the actions of their parents. As we have noted, the idea of the earthly evidence of grace is still very much alive in our culture. Thus, although Edith Wharton does not explain this mechanism in her novel, we recognize it unconsciously, and her use of it adds greatly to its emotional impact upon us.

THE TRAGIC HERO: Edith Wharton also uses the narrator to establish the uniqueness of Ethan Frome, which makes him a character with whom we can identify and sympathize. This is accomplished subtly, through the comments that the engineer makes throughout the first part of his story. His first description of Ethan introduces the hero as "the most striking figure in Starkfield, though he was but the ruin of a man." We learn that Ethan is very tall, that he had a "careless powerful look" in spite of "a lameness checking each step like the jerk of a chain." (We can also appreciate the brilliance of this last image, which tells us explicitly that Ethan is imprisoned by an invisible power.) The engineer also tells us that even Ethan's "indifferent" neighbors (who had troubles enough of their own) conceded that his troubles "had been beyond the common measure." Obviously, he is a special person.

Ethan's lameness is also a significant symbol in the novel beyond its importance as a sign of his punishment. Whether or not Mrs. Wharton intended it, his lameness corresponds to a characteristic of the priest-kings of the early Greek culture, who were often ham-strung, or lamed for various reasons. This characteristic was used in the Greek plays, where the prince or king often wore a high-heeled shoe to indicate his lameness, and therefore his kingliness, and thus identify himself to the audience. Even today, we are distressed in the presense of a severely crippled person, in part, perhaps, because his condition seems like a threat to our own physical wholeness. Thus, both in the present, and in its echo of a past meaning, Ethan's lameness adds to the charged quality of his person.

THE TRAGIC FLAW: There is one other aspect of the convention of the tragic hero which the author uses. This is the hero's "tragic flaw." While the formal tragedy uses the force of fate as the primary force that pushes the hero toward the

tragic act, the convention requires that the hero have a moment of choice—but it is a moment that he cannot use to save
himself because of a factor in his own makeup. This element
is very important in the type of work that *Ethan Frome* represents, because without it he would not have that dignity which
humanity attributes to itself—the dignity of choice. Instead, he
would be merely the "child of circumstance," a cliche which
reflects the idea that only a child has no choice in his condition; a man can make his own. Thus, in all formal tragedies,
there is a moment, just before the end, when the hero is con-
fronted with a means of escape. In *Ethan Frome*, this moment
comes when Ethan decides to ask the contractor, Andrew
Hale, for an advance on the large load of lumber he has de-
livered to him. Since the advance would be enough for him
to take Mattie away to the West, this constitutes a real attempt
at freedom.

But now we are presented with a subtle exposition of the use
of the tragic flaw. In Ethan, it is his pride. On his way to
Hale's, the author gives us hope that he will forego it: how
much, she asks, "did pride count in the ebullition of feelings
in his breast?" But when he meets Mrs. Hale on the way, he
seizes upon her words of sympathy as an excuse to give up his
attempt. Instead of having Ethan say that he cannot face the
loss of pride that his request would entail, the author has him
see himself as someone who was trying to take advantage of
the Hales' sympathy to obtain money on false pretenses. Thus
Ethan's choice is made, and the fateful consequences must
follow.

A STUDY IN CONTRAST: The character of Ethan Frome is
also brought into relief by contrast with the character of the
successful Irish grocer's son, Denis Eady. Eady is everything
that Frome is not. He is of foreign stock, in contrast to Ethan,
whose family has long been in New England. Thus Eady does
not bear the burden of Starkfield's history of poverty and sickness. On the contrary we learn that his father's "suppleness
and effrontery had given Starkfield its first notion of 'smart'
business methods" and that he had been very successful. Obviously, there is no sin in the Eady household. Where Ethan
is stiff—and later, lame—Eady is agile and easy. For example,

the first time Eady appears he is described as "a young man with a sprightly foot." When we next see him, through the church windows, he "danced well," whirling Mattie around the floor in a Virginia reel "in circles of increasing swiftness." Where Ethan is formal and finds words difficult, Eady is familiar, even—as seen through Ethan's jealous eyes—impudent. For example, we have Eady's easy banter as he tries to get Mattie to join him in his "cutter" after the dance, contrasted with Ethan's long, thoughtful silences and the awkwardness of Ethan's speeches as he takes Mattie home. Even their horses are opposites: Eady drives a young roan colt, while Ethan drives a hollow-backed bay.

The fact of Eady's father's success through modern business methods and its contrast to the poverty and traditional ways of Ethan and many of his neighbors is also important to the story. It is as if the New England way of life, with its dark, Puritanical outlook, had something of evil in it. There is also an intimation that the good life is only in the present, in the modern world. This is underscored at one point by the engineer, from whom we learn that Ethan was once interested in engineering himself. It is obvious that interest in the modern world is connected with better times. The fact that the narrator is an engineer—someone from another world than the tradition-bound universe of Starkfield—is also significant.

Returning once more to the Greek parallel, it is interesting to note how Edith Wharton emphasizes the importance of the post office, and how she specifies the nature of Ethan's mail. "It you know Starkfield," she says, "you know the post-office." And it is in front of the post office that we first see Ethan Frome, dragging himself to the white colannade. If we consider Ethan Frome against the background of the Greek plays (in which we know Edith Wharton was steeped in childhood) we can see him as an echo of a supplicant, dragging himself toward the white colonnade of a Greek temple to consult the oracle (a priest acting as the voice of the residing deity). This type of scene is often described by the chorus or enacted (as in Sophocles' *Oedipus the King*). But the oracle has no news for Ethan. Each day he only receives a copy of the *Bettsbridge Eagle*, a newspaper form a neighboring town, and occasionally there is an advertisement for a patent medicine for his wife. Nothing changes.

NATURE AS SIN: The fate of Ethan, as well as of Mattie, also lies in the nature of Mattie herself. It is her passionate nature that enchants Ethan and it is at her urging that they attempt suicide. Her role as an enchantress is indicated several times throughout the story. For example, when we first see her, through Ethan's eyes, she is wearing a cherry-colored "fascinator"—a gauzy scarf—around her head. To her quality of enchantment Edith Wharton has added the image of a moon goddess, an image which is clearly intended on two occasions. The first is when Frome is watching her dance through the window, when he catches sight of "the cloud of dark hair about her forehead," like a cloud across the moon. Again, on the night they spend together alone while Zeena is away, Mattie walks before Ethan, carrying a candle so that its light makes "her dark hair look like a drift of mist on the moon." Her name is also Silver, the color of the moon.

Of course, in Puritan New England, there is no such thing as a moon goddess or a child of nature. There is only the good child or the bad seed; only the good woman or the witch. To the modern eye, these two may be hard to differentiate, but in Ethan's world, they are as distinct as the saved and the damned. Mattie's inclinations in this respect serve to notify us that she will come to no good, for we are in a world where the Puritan image still predominates.

A MOURNFUL PRIVILEGE: The fact that this close contact with nature finally forms the bond between Ethan and Mattie, a contact which they both share, therefore means that this bond itself is doomed. It is this quality in Mattie that changes Ethan's attitude toward her, so that where he at first resents having to walk Mattie home from town affairs because it means an extra four-mile walk after a hard day, he comes to wish that "Starkfield might give all its nights to revelry." Ethan's sensitivity to nature and its significance is made explicit by the author in the statement: "He had always been more sensitive than the people about him to the appeal of natural beauty." We also learn that even in his unhappiest moments, "field and sky spoke to him with a deep and powerful persuasion." Yet until Mattie came, the author tells us that this sensibility only served to increase his sense of separateness, as if he were "the sole victim of this mournful privilege." In the last statement we see the Puritan attitude underlined: a sensitivity to nature is not admissible; it is a secret thing that is not normally shared with others because there is something wrong with having it; in fact, those who have it are in a sense victims.

The intensity of his response to the recognition that Mattie, too, was subject to this strange sensitivity is made very clear by the author. She tells us how he saw Mattie as that "one other spirit (who) trembled with the same touch of wonder." In keeping with the idea of the love of nature as a forbidden thing, Edith Wharton has Ethan tell Mattie of the stars whose very names are pagan, and of prehistoric times, a time when nature was all. She describes the undefinable sensations which "drew them together with a shock of joy" in the presence of the "cold red of sunset" or the flight of cloud shadows over the fields. Yet even here there is a sudden, subtly false note which seems to be intended to show the depth to which Ethan's spiritual solitude had brought him. In a moment of intense feeling, Mattie says "It looks just as if it was painted!" The author then tells us that this pathetically prosaic phrase sounded to Ethan like the end of the art of definition, and that he felt that "words had at last been found to utter his secret soul." It is possible, of course, that Edith Wharton thought Mattie's phrase charming, but one tends to give her more credit than that.

A FOOT IN BOTH WORLDS: There is another aspect of Mattie which is important in the story: it is the fact that despite her circumstances, she has a degree of choice, because although she has one foot in Ethan's forbidden world, the other is set, however delicately, in the acceptable world of the Protestant community. This is made very clear in the first chapter of the story, where her presence in the warmth and happiness in the church among the townfolk at the dance is sharply contrasted with Ethan's lonely presence outside it, looking in through the windows like a hungry child in a fairy tale might look into the window of a house where a feast was taking place. Edith Wharton's description of Ethan as he virtually sneaks up to the church is masterful. He "skirts" the side of the building; he "keeps out of the range of the revealing rays from within"; he hugs the shadow and edges his way forward cautiously. The entire paragraph describes, not a member of the town, but an outcast, a pariah, one who not only does not belong, but who does not even dare to be seen there. The contrast between his situation and that of those within is also clearly stated. He stands in "pure and frosty darkness," while the interior of the church seethes "in a mist of heat." Mattie, on the other hand, is not only one of the people—she "passes down the line," she swings "from hand to hand" among them—but she is singled out to start the dance by the most alive of the living—Denis Eady. As a person, she is accepted by this world. For example, Mrs. Hale says of Mattie as she was before the "accident": "I never knew a sweeter nature." And again, speaking of her appearance in Ethan's lonely existence, the author describes her as "a hopeful young life."

A SUDDEN GIRL: Nevertheless, the balance is weighted for Mattie on the side of death, not life. As we have noted, she is imprisoned by poverty, and she carries within herself a love of nature—in fact, the author has virtually identified her with it, as the moon. But the author has also given her another attribute which we finally come to realize as a prophetic element: it is her capacity for sudden and complete changes of mood. The author uses this characteristic brilliantly. The first time we are made aware of it is when Mattie and Ethan are talking of the danger of the big elm at the foot of the hill, and Ethan's skill in steering the sleigh to avoid it. This time, the author has Mattie assert casually that she is not afraid, and then suddenly walk rapidly, grimly onward. The second time is when, standing at the top of the hill in despair and defeat at their parting, she suddenly throws her arms around Ethan's neck and begs him to take her coasting down the hill, "right into the big elm. . . . So 't we'd never have to leave each other any more."

Thus it is Mattie who by the power of her passionate nature and her "suddenness" brings Ethan to commit the tragic act.

This element of suddenness is thus very important. Knowing Ethan and his meditative side, we also know that he would not have done it if he had had time to think about it. But Mattie's capacity for sudden change, the bond between them, and Mattie's sudden avowal that she shared his feelings were too much for Ethan to resist. The author, however, makes Ethan's motivation even stronger by contrasting Ethan's sudden sense of fulfillment with the vision of Zeena and his life with her. She writes that "Mattie's avowal . . . made the other vision more abhorrent, . . . more intolerable to return to." At that point Ethan's mind is made up.

TWO TALES ON ONE THEME: As we have noted earlier, the entire affair between Mattie and Ethan and its final outcome echoes the story of Paolo and Francesca in the *Divine Comedy*. This does not lessen the value of Edith Wharton's story; rather, her use of Dante's tale enriches *Ethan Frome* by setting the echoes of the old story to reverberate through the new. We can read Ethan and Mattie's story in many lines of Dante. For example, Francesca says: "Love, which lies smoldering in each gentle heart,/Inflamed him for the beauty that was mine." This certainly describes Ethan's situation as we find it in the novel. Then she says: "Love, that will take for answer only love,/Caught me so fiercely up in his delight/That, as you see, he still is by my side./Love led us to one death." Here we have the elements of Ethan and Mattie's lover's suicide and their continued unity in Hell. She continues: "One day . . . we read the book/of Launcelot, and how love conquered him./. . . From time to time our eyes would . . . meet to kindle blushes in our cheeks./ . . . When we were reading how those smiling lips/Were kissed by such a lover,—Paolo here,/Who never more from me shall be divided,/All trembling, held and kissed me on the mouth./ . . . On that day we read no more."

The love story that sets the tone for Paolo and Francesca has its approximate counterpart in *Ethan Frome* in the presence of Mattie's friend, Ruth Varnum, and her fiance, Ned Hale. By introducing this happy couple into the novel, Edith Wharton has again used the technique of bringing a situation into sharp relief by presenting its antithesis. As the character of Denis Eady serves to make the character of Ethan clearer to the reader, so the presence of a happy, legitimately engaged couple serves to set off the unhappy illegitimacy of Ethan and Mattie's relationship. This contrast is made all the more stark by the way in which we are first informed of Ned and Ruth's existence, when Mattie says: that they "came just as *near* running into the big elm at the bottom. We were all sure they were killed." The happy couple, however, merely had a close shave. Ethan and Mattie's encounter with the elm was another matter.

KISS AND CONSEQUENCE: The precipitating effect of the kiss of the ideal couple (in the book in Dante and in the person of Ruth and Ned in *Ethan Frome*) is also used in the scene where Ethan and Mattie are alone together after Zeena has left for the night. But here, as for the rest of Dante's story, the correspondence is established by contrast rather than by similarity. The kiss is of course the kiss of Ruth and Ned that Ethan awkwardly mentions in an attempt at pleasantry. But instead of bringing them together, Ethan's mention of the kiss makes Mattie withdraw. The lovemaking that is so eloquently implied by the last line of Paolo's story is reflected by its *absence* in *Ethan Frome*. Edith Wharton has given this scene a highly charged quality by creating all the conditions for lovemaking—two people, passionately in love, alone in an isolated farmhouse before a cozy fire—and then having no love made, not even a kiss exchanged. On the one hand we see the power of the lover's environment which restrains them even under these circumstances, when they are already so far beyond the pale.

The extent to which they pass beyond their convention is cleverly intimated by the author when she describes how the room became quiet as the two sat after supper, Mattie with her sewing and Ethan with his pipe, and how "all constraint had vanished between the two." But the full depth of the fantasy that encloses the pair is stated more explicitly when the author notes Ethan's "illusion of long-established intimacy" and how he "set his imagination adrift on the fiction that they had always spent their evenings thus and would always go on doing so. . . ." Thus, while no physical lovemaking takes place, we realize that Ethan's submission to his fantasy is its symbolic equivalent in Puritan terms, and that in effect, the deed has been done. When Ethan is finally roused from his fantasy by the sight of Zeena's rocking chair and thinks, "I've been in a dream, and this is the only evening we'll ever have together," it is too late. Only by moving to a land where fantasy is not a crime could he escape his fate. But as we know, he foregoes that possibility.

Before we leave the parallels between Dante's and Edith Wharton's tales, we might also note that the tenor of the affairs between the pairs of lovers is identical. There is the same shyness and the lack of verbal acknowledgement—"From time to time our eyes would meet/To kindle blushes in our cheeks"—until the very end, when the fatal step is taken. Ethan and Mattie's actual kiss does not, of course, come until just before they attempt suicide, but the ultimate result is the same in both cases, since both suicides have the same genesis and purpose.

THE POWER OF ZEENA: In our appreciation of the structure and execution of the story of Ethan Frome, we have yet to deal with the way Edith Wharton has created and used the character of Zeena Frome, Ethan's wife. She is unquestionably the most powerful character in the novel, and it is she who in effect determines the action. It is Zeena who decides that Ethan should walk Mattie home from town affairs, and who thus throws them together for the long walks in which their common sensitivity to nature becomes evident. It is she who creates the conditions where the lovers are left alone for the night when she goes off to consult a "new doctor." And it is she who precipitates their suicide attempt when she summarily sends Mattie away. As she is presented in the book, her power in her small world of Ethan and Mattie is awesome. Although she says little, the cloud of her silent disapproval hangs over the household. Both Ethan and Mattie walk in her presence as if they were walking on eggshells, fearful to call her "disfavor" down upon themselves. While her capacity to make Ethan miserable had existed before Mattie came, the author makes clear that the real source of her power in the novel lies in the fact that she has the power to send Mattie away, because

Mattie is *her* relative, not Ethan's. When she finally exercises this power, its effect is like an execution of a judgment.

From the first time that the author introduces us to Zeena, she is associated with sickness and death. For example, our first knowledge of her are the patent-medicine advertisements that the engineer sees Ethan pick up at the post office. The second mention of her is that she is "sickly," the outward reason for all her actions in the story is based in her perpetual sickness. Even her first meeting with Ethan is brought about by illness, when she comes to nurse his mother until her death. And in the end, it is the invaliding of Mattie which qualifies the latter to return to the household, enabling Zeena to express her power in "doctoring."

ZEENA THE WITCH: The sickliness of Zeena Frome, however, is just one aspect of a personality which the author paints in the darkest spectral terms. There is little doubt that although she remains within the Puritan convention, and even perhaps because of it, Zeena is really a ghostly witch. Edith Wharton makes this clear in a hundred ways throughout the novel. Her first speech (when Ethan is dressing in the dark winter morning) is made in the dark, like the unexpected voice of a ghost. Like a ghost, Ethan sees her as indistinctly outlined. The author makes her second appearance even more spectral. As Zeena opens the door for Ethan and Mattie when they return from the church dance, she stands "tall and angular, one hand drawing a quilted counterpane to her flat breast, while the other held a lamp." The description makes the quality of apparition even stronger by detailing how the light picks out her puckered throat, her clutching hand on the quilt, and deepens "fantastically" the hollows of her high boned face. Obviously, this is a woman from whom no good can come.

There is one brief indication that the atmosphere of Starkfield itself is responsible for Zeena's transformation from a talkative, efficient nurse, "the very genius of health," into the silent, ailing creature of the novel. The author offers the suggestion that her change might be due to the effect of life on the farm in a neighborhood which contained many houses "where stricken creatures pined." But, she quickly points out, Zeena's "sickliness" had made her notable "even in a community rich in pathological instances." Thus, while Starkfield has undoubtedly taken its toll, Zeena is not an ordinary hypochondriac.

THE POWER OF SILENCE: The power of Zeena's silence, its charged quality, and its effect on Ethan and Mattie is also made clear. Her silence to Ethan, the author says, seemed "deliberately assumed to conceal far-reaching intentions, mysterious conclusions drawn from suspicions and resentments impossible to guess." And to Mattie, her silence is also puzzling and frightening, particularly since she is totally dependent upon Zeena. "I can see she ain't suited, and yet I don't know why," she cries to Ethan.

Only once in the novel does this silent conflict which Zeena creates break into open hostility. Even though the exchange— where Zeena and Ethan argue about sending Mattie away— is strong, the author indicates the even stronger emotional level at which it is taking place, and how it is heightened by the early evening darkness which surrounds them. She describes how in "the obscurity which hid their faces their thoughts seemed to dart at each other like serpents shooting venom." (Here is an excellent example of the inadequacy of the author's language. While the depth of the conflict is certainly implied, the cliché quality of "serpents shooting venom" dulls the full power of the emotional quality which a more poetic writer might have achieved.)

But Ethan cannot win against his unscrupulous adversary, partly because of his own guilt, but also because of his pride. He views the argument as "senseless and savage," as a physical fight and is filled with "shame" at his own share in it. Basically it is his pride that makes him vulnerable, and the power of the Puritan idea that holds feeling in abhorrence only tends to throw him back upon his own weakness even more.

THE CAT AND THE PICKLE DISH: But the character and power of Zenobia Frome, and particularly her witch-like quality, is most cleverly expressed by the author through the use she makes of Zeena's cat. For example, in the scene where

Mattie and Ethan are alone together, the cat manages to break Zeena's treasured and forbidden pickle dish which Mattie has set out for their supper. By this symbolic act, the author accomplishes several things. In the first place, the dish is apparently sacred to Zeena, since we know that she got it from her "aunt that married the minister," and that "she never meant it should be used." The intimation is that some kind of desecration has occurred. Secondly, Ethan and Mattie's fear and concern over the broken dish emphasize the fact that this is Zeena's house, not Mattie's, and the reader is made aware of the discrepancy. Thirdly, the author establishes the cat as Zeena's ally and representative, for the animal has provided its mistress with irrefutable evidence of the events of that evening.

The cat as Zeena-the-witch's familiar is skillfully used by the author throughout the rest of the scene. It sits in Zeena's chair, "watching them with narrowed eyes," as if Zeena herself were watching. And finally, when it jumps off the chair to go after a mouse: "as a result of its sudden movement the empty chair . . . set up a spectral rocking," it reminds Ethan of Zeena's reality and wakes him from his evening's fantasy with Mattie.

CRITICAL COMMENTARY

Since many literary critics agree that *Ethan Frome* is among Edith Wharton's finest and most important works, any major criticism of Mrs. Wharton must necessarily have reference to her famous tale of the New England farmer, Ethan Frome, his sickly wife, Zenobia, and the young relative, Mattie Silver. The first part of this summary of criticism deals with important references to Mrs. Wharton and her entire work, which should help one toward a better understanding of *Ethan Frome*. The second part is concerned especially with studies, which contain special references to this particular work of fiction. The third part is a discussion of a dramatization of *Ethan Frome*.

IMPORTANT GENERAL CRITICISM. This aspect of the criticism will be subdivided into seven parts: (1) book-length studies of Mrs. Wharton and her works; (2) briefer, specific studies of Mrs. Wharton's works; (3) Mrs. Wharton's life; (4) Mrs. Wharton placed in perspective with other novelists; (5) studies of Mrs. Wharton in relation to one other literary figure (or a cluster of figures); (6) moral qualities in Mrs. Wharton's works; and (7) studies of Mrs. Wharton's art.

(1) BOOK-LENGTH STUDIES OF MRS. WHARTON AND HER WORKS. With the passage of time, the longer studies of Mrs. Wharton have become more and more worthwhile. In 1922, Katharine F. Gerould brought out a comparatively brief treatment, entitled *Edith Wharton: A Critical Study*. In 1925, Robert M. Lovett produced the first of the important detailed studies, *Edith Wharton*. This monograph (a small book) is a thoughtful examination of Mrs. Wharton's life to date, her novels, the development of her literary reputation, and the method of her art. It has some thoughtful references to Henry James and Thackeray, both of whom Edith Wharton admired. Ten years after Mrs. Wharton died (in 1937), Percy Lubbock, an English friend of the novelist, published a biographical work entitled *A Portrait of Edith Wharton* (1947). This work has very little space devoted to critical aspects of the literary works. One highlight of the work is Mr. Lubbock's weaving together of reminiscent sketches (written at his request by numerous of Mrs. Wharton's friends). A romanticized picture of the artist is presented, emphasizing her appeal to her European friends, especially Henry James. A weakness of this partial portrait is the omission of the American side of Mrs. Wharton's background and development. An outstanding, long critical work is an analysis and appreciation of Mrs. Wharton's works, *Edith Wharton: A Study of Her Fiction,* published in 1953 by Blake Nevius. The sympathetic criticism of her works and art is worthwhile, and the discussion of her major themes is excellent. She is carefully placed in perspective with her literary contemporaries. In the Twentieth Century Views Series, there is a splendid little book entitled *Edith Wharton: A Collection of Critical Essays* (1962), edited by Irving Howe. This volume includes commentaries by leading authorities on Edith Wharton and her art, as well as evaluations of her novels in general and some single works in particular. A helpful composite picture of the artist is assembled. Mrs. Wharton herself has written two books which throw much light on her work. *The Writing of Fiction* (1925), a work of literary criticism, points up her artistic beliefs. *A Backward Glance* (1934), her autobiography, contains much background information about her childhood and early married life in America, as well as accounts of her friends and travels in Europe. Millicent Bell's *Edith Wharton and Henry James: The Story of Their Friendship* (1965) offers some very interesting new material on Mrs. Wharton. The book is based essentially upon fifty-seven letters, representing such people as Henry James, Gaillard Lapsley, W. C. Brownell, Walter Berry, and the Charles Eliot Nortons. One sees a picture of the middle part of Mrs. Wharton's life, especially her European experiences, her travels, her dinner parties, her friendships, and the thoughts confided to intimate friends— the time of the last years of her marriage and her divorce. The whole treatment is sympathetic. Louis Auchincloss's *The Edith Wharton Reader* (1965) is a very worthwhile collection of excerpts from Mrs. Wharton's finest work. Particularly of interest are the "Introduction" and the "Prefatory Note" for each of the varied selections. Probably the two most useful of these longer studies are Blake Nevius' careful literary *Study* (for measured criticism) and Mrs. Wharton's own sensitive autobiography (for a partial picture of her life).

(2) BRIEFER, CRITICAL STUDIES OF MRS. WHARTON'S WORKS.

Six early critical articles concerning the works (listed chronologically) are as follows: Anna M. Sholl's "The Work of Edith Wharton," *Gunton's* (1903); Henry D. Sedgwick's "The Novels of Mrs. Wharton," *Atlantic Monthly* (1906); H. G. Dwight's "The Work of Mrs. Wharton," *Putnam's* (1908); F. T. Cooper's "Critical Study of Mrs. Wharton," *Some American Story Tellers* (1911); Edwin A. Bjorkman's "The Greater Edith Wharton," *Voices of To-Morrow* (1913); and, Percy Lubbock's "The Novels of Edith Wharton," *Quarterly Review* (1915). (The last two items are particularly good for critical estimates of the works.) Some outstanding brief critical commentaries concerning Mrs. Wharton's works published in the 1920's and 1930's are these: Percy H. Boynton's "Edith Wharton," *English Journal* (1923); Joseph Collins' *Taking the Literary Pulse: Psychological Studies of Life and Letters* (1924); Grant Overton's *Authors of the Day* (1924); Stuart P. Sherman's "Edith Wharton: Costuming the Passions," *The Main Stream* (1927); Van Meter Ames's "The Technique of the Novel," *Aesthetics of the Novel* (1928); Grant Overton's *The Women Who Make Our Novels* (1928); Grant Overton's *An Hour of the American Novel* (1929); Fred Lewis Pattee's "The Feminine Novel," *The New American Literature* (1930); Robert Sencourt's "The Poetry of Edith Wharton," *Bookman* (1931); Joseph Warren Beach's *The Twentieth-Century Novel: Studies in Technique* (1932); Frances Russell's "Edith Wharton's Use of Imagery," *English Journal* (1932); Frances Russell's "Melodramatic Mrs. Wharton," *Sewanee Review* (1932); E.K. Brown's "Mrs. Wharton," in Pelham Edgar's *The Art of the Novel from 1700 to the Present Time* (1933); Bertha Coolidge's "Mrs. Wharton's Works," *Saturday Review of Literature* (1933); Harlan H. Hatcher's "Realism and the Public Taste: 1900-1921," *Creating the Modern American Novel* (1935); Christopher D. Morley's *Streamlines* (1936); John Crowe Ransom's "Characters and Character," *American Review* (1936); M. Lawrence's "Helpmeets," *School of Femininity* (1936); E. K.

Brown's "Edith Wharton," *Etudes Anglaises* (1938); and Q. D. Leavis' "Henry James' Heiress: The Importance of Edith Wharton," *Scrutiny* (1938). (The Collins and Pattee listings include some especially worthwhile comments on the works.) After Mrs. Wharton's death in 1937, the critics began to survey her entire literary contribution. Two comprehensive surveys were published in 1952: Edward Wagenknecht's "Edith Wharton: Social Background and Ethical Dilemma," *Cavalcade of the American Novel;* and Anne Fremantle's "Edith Wharton: Values and Vulgarity," in Harold C. Gardiner, S.J., ed., *Fifty Years of the American Novel: A Christian Appraisal.* These were followed, in 1954, by John Harvey's interesting essay, "Contrasting Worlds, A Study in the Novels of Edith Wharton," *Etudes Anglaises.* "These Are Sturdy Tales" is a brief article of some interest in the August 18, 1958 issue of *Newsweek.* Nancy R. Leach's article, "Edith Wharton's Unpublished Novel," *American Literature* (1953), catches the attention of a thoroughgoing Wharton fan.

(3) MRS. WHARTON'S LIFE.   Six worthy references to Mrs. Wharton's life (all published before her death in 1937) are as follows: Francis W. Halsey's "Women Authors of Our Day in Their Homes" (1903); R. Herrick's "Mrs. Wharton's World," *New Republic* (1915); Percy H. Boynton's "Edith Wharton," *English Journal* (1923); Stanley J. Kunitz, ed., *Living Authors* (1931); E. Carroll's "Visit With Edith Wharton," *Delineator* (1932); and Harlan H. Hatcher's "Realism and the Public Taste," 1900-1921," *Creating the Modern American Novel* (1935).

Twelve biographical articles, all entitled "Portrait," have been published in the *Woman's Home Companion* (1919), in the *Literary Digest* (1922 and 1923), in the *Literary Review* (1924), in *Mentor* (1927 and 1929), in the *Journal* (1930), in *Bookman* (1932)), in the *Saturday Review of Literature* (1944, and June and May, 1952), and in the *Publisher's Weekly* (1950). In the year of Edith Wharton's death (1937), Henry S. Canby's article, "Edith Wharton," was in the *Saturday Review of Literature.* Mrs. Wharton's "Obituary," appearing in several periodicals, is of biographical interest:

Commonwealth (August 27, 1937); *Newsweek* (August 21, 1937); *Publishers' Weekly* (August 21, 1937); and *Time* (August 23, 1937). In the following year, 1938, Edmund Wilson presents a very stimulating survey and commentary concerning Mrs. Wharton's major works in an article called "Justice to Edith Wharton," *The New Republic*. (Mr. Wilson suggests that her most valuable work began with *The House of Mirth*, 1905, and ended with *The Age of Innocence*, 1920.) A few years later, in 1946, James Gray includes Mrs. Wharton in an article, "Very Important Personages," in a book entitled *On Second Thought*. In the 1950's, two articles treated Mrs. Wharton's life: Edmund Wilson's "A Memoir of Edith Wharton," *Classics and Commercials* (1950); and Van Wyck Brooks' "Edith Wharton," *The Confident Years*: 1885-1915 (1952). Michael Swan has surveyed "The Early Edith Wharton," *A Small Part of Time* (1961), and Louis Auchincloss has presented a workmanlike study entitled *Edith Wharton* (1961), one of the University of Minnesota Pamphlets on American Writers.

(4) MRS. WHARTON PLACED IN PERSPECTIVE WITH OTHER NOVELISTS. Six works (listed here chronologically) treat Mrs. Wharton as a person and a literary artist seen against a background of other writers: Carl Van Doren's *Contemporary American Novelists* (1922); Grant Overton's *Authors of the Day* (1924); Percy H. Boynton's *Some Contemporary Americans* (1924); Paul Green and Elizabeth L. Green's *Contemporary American Literature*: *A Study of Fourteen Outstanding American Writers* (1925); Sir John C. Squire and others, *Contemporary American Authors* (1928); and Grant Overton's *The Women Who Make Our Novels* (1928). In the 1930's, three outstanding histories of American letters precisely place Mrs. Wharton among other prominent American novelists: Harry Hartwick's *The Foreground of American Fiction* (1934); Walter F. Taylor's *History of American Letters* (1936); and Arthur Hobson Quinn's *American Fiction*: *An Historical and Critical Survey* (1936). Four commentaries, published since Mrs. Wharton's death, include a more complete evaluation of her comparative placement. They are (chronologically listed) as follows: Carl Van Doren's "Tra-

dition and Transition," *The American Novel: 1789-1939*
(1940); Fred B. Millett's *Contemporary American Authors*
(1940); George Snell's *Shapers of American Fiction* (1947);
and Frederick Hoffman's *The Modern Novel in America: 1900-
1950* (1951).

**(5) STUDIES OF MRS. WHARTON IN RELATION TO ONE OTHER
LITERARY FIGURE (OR A CLUSTER OF FIGURES).** A number
of stimulating articles have been written analyzing Mrs.
Wharton with one other comparable literary figure, or as
one of a small, selected group of artists. The following three
works discuss Edith Wharton in connection with other women
writers only: Joseph Collins's "Big Four of American Women
Writers," *Taking the Literary Pulse: Psychological Studies of
Life and Letters* (1924); George Snell's "Edith Wharton and
Willa Cather," *The Shapers of American Fiction: 1798-1947*
(1947); Josephine Lurie Jessup's *The Faith of Our Feminists:
A Study of the Novels of Edith Wharton, Ellen Glasgow,
Willa Cather* (1950); and Louis Auchincloss's *Pioneers and
Caretakers: A Study of Nine American Novelists* (1965). Mr.
Auchincloss discusses Mrs. Wharton's ability to write well-
constructed novels which include some unattractive pictures
of both male and female characters. He further writes of
women as being "the true conservatives." Since the time of
her death (1937), four articles connect Edith Wharton with
one or more male writers of fiction: Q. D. Leavis' "Henry
James's Heiress: The Importance of Edith Wharton," *Scrutiny* (1938); Alfred Kazin's "Two Educations: Edith Wharton
and Theodore Dreiser," *On Native Grounds* (1942) (Mr.
Kazin writes of Mrs. Wharton as one who helps to represent
American literature properly since 1900); Frederick H. Hoffman's "Points of Moral Reference: A Compromise Study of
Edith Wharton and F. Scott Fitzgerald," *English Institute
Essays* (1949); and Blanche H. Gelfant's "Sherwood Anderson, Edith Wharton, and Thomas Wolfe," *The American City
Novel* (1954). Two writers of fiction (one male and one
female) have commented on Mrs. Wharton and her art: Henry
James in *Notes on Novelists* (1914); and Katherine Mansfield
in *Novels and Novelists* (1930). Edith Wharton herself has
written four articles about literary figures she admires (who

possibly have influenced her thought or style): "George
Eliot," *Bookman* (1902); "Marcel Proust," *Yale Review* (1925);
"Reconsideration of Proust," *Saturday Review of Literature*
(1934); and "William C. Brownell," *Scribner's* (1928). An
interesting article concerned with Mrs. Wharton's correspond-
ence with a literary friend is Hilda Fife's "Letters from Edith
Wharton to Vernon Lee," *Colby Library Quarterly* (1953).
(Vernon Lee is the pen name of Miss Violet Paget, author of
Studies of the Eighteenth Century in Italy, much admired
by Mrs. Wharton.)

(6) MORAL QUALITIES IN MRS. WHARTON'S WORKS. Edith
Wharton's concern with the moral point of view is noted in
the following three articles (listed chronologically)—the first
being an early criticism, and the other two representing her
attitude within a few years of her death: Charles Waldstein's
"Social Ideals," *North American Review* (1906); Catherine
Gilbertson's "Mrs. Wharton, an Agate Lamp Within Thy
Hand," *Century* (1929); and J. C. Ransom's "Characters and
Character," *American Review* (1936). In 1934, Mrs. Wharton
herself published in the *Saturday Review of Literature* a use-
ful essay entitled "Permanent Values in Fiction." Three books
have interesting chapters with references to some of Edith
Wharton's ideas on moral values: Nellie E. Monroe's "Moral
Situation in Edith Wharton," *Novel and Society* (1941);
Edward C. Wagenknecht's "Edith Wharton: Social Back-
ground and Ethical Dilemma," *Cavalcade of the American
Novel* (1952); and H. Wayne Morgan's "Edith Wharton: The
Novelist of Manners and Morals," *Writers in Transition: Seven
Americans* (1963). Four comparatively recent doctoral dis-
sertations (all written since Mrs. Wharton's death in 1937)
emphasize this important aspect of her literary work. Listed
chronologically, they are as follows: Rod W. Horton's "Social
and Individual Values in the New York Stories of Edith
Wharton," New York University (1945); Mary Lund Rice's
"The Moral Conservatism of Edith Wharton," University of
Minnesota (1953); Thomas Saunder's "Moral Values in the
Novels of Edith Wharton," University of Pittsburgh (1954);
and M. J. Lyde's "The Theory and Treatment of Morality
in the Work of Edith Wharton," University of Chicago (1956).

Millicent Bell's recent book-length biographical study, *Edith Wharton and Henry James: The Story of Their Friendship* (1965), is rich with references to Mrs. Wharton's own sensitive moral qualities and firm integrity of character. (Some of her personal life is very likely reflected in her fiction; for example, parts of *The Reef* (1912) could be interpreted as somewhat autobiographical.)

(7) STUDIES OF MRS. WHARTON'S ART. Much has been written about Mrs. Wharton's literary technique and philosophy. The following six comparatively early studies are of some interest to one investigating the beginning phases of her work: Henry D. Sedgwick's "The Art of Mrs. Wharton," *The New American Type and Other Essays* (1908); H. W. Boynton's "Mrs. Wharton's Manner," *Nation* (1913); John C. Underwood's "Culture and Edith Wharton," *Literature and Insurgency* (1914); "Edith Wharton: Two Conflicting Estimates of Her Art," *Current Opinion* (1915); F. Hackett's "Mrs. Wharton's Art," *New Republic* (1917); and Helen Thomas Follett and Wilson Follett's "Edith Wharton," *Some Modern Novelists: Appreciations and Estimates* (1919). (The Sedgwick and Underwood items are especially good for general criticism, and the Folletts' offering is particularly worthwhile for a discussion of Mrs. Wharton's technique and general philosophy.) Five articles of the late 1920's and the early 1930's further one's knowledge of Edith Wharton's technique: Stuart P. Sherman's "Edith Wharton: Costuming the Passions," *The Main Stream* (1927); Frances T. Russell's "Edith Wharton's Use of Imagery," *English Journal* (1932); Joseph Warren Beach's *The Twentieth-Century Novel: Studies in Technique* (1932); Frances T. Russell's "Melodramatic Mrs. Wharton," *Sewanee Review* (1932); and E. K. Brown's "Mrs. Wharton," in Pelham Edgar's *The Art of the Novel from 1700 to the Present Time* (1933). (The Russell listings are of specialized interest; the Beach work is a distinguished study.) Since Mrs. Wharton's death (beginning with the early 1950's and continuing through to the present time), there have been a number of very good critical commentaries published: Edward Wagenknecht's "Affirmation: Of Art and of Life," *Cavalcade of the American Novel* (1952), is worthwhile. Winifred Lynskey's "The 'Heroes' of Edith Wharton," *University of Toronto Quarterly* (1954), is helpful. L. O. Coxe's "What Edith Wharton Saw in Innocence," *New Republic* (1955), is very sensitive in the exploration of meaning in Mrs. Wharton's works (especially *The Age of Innocence,* 1920). Norman Friedman's "Point of View in Fiction: The Development of a Critical Concept," *Publications of the Modern Language Association* (1955), is excellent in helping a reader decide what method (or combination of methods) of storytelling is being followed. M. J. Lyde's *Edith Wharton: Convention and Morality in the Work of a Novelist* (1959) offers a detailed analysis of Mrs. Wharton's philosophy. Irving Howe's "The Achievement of Edith Wharton" is the keynote essay in his collected group of studies entitled *Edith Wharton: A Collection of Critical Essays* (1962). (This essay has very helpful and provocative subheadings, such as "The Range of Her Achievement," "The Heiress of Henry James?" and "A Personal Vision.") Millicent Bell's *Edith Wharton and Henry James: The Story of Their Friendship* (1965) interestingly suggests that within Mrs. Wharton's own experiences may be found sources for plotting and characterization for some of her works. Two rather recent studies present different points of view about Mrs. Wharton's approach to the novel: Larry Rubin's "Aspects of Naturalism in Four Novels by Edith Wharton," *Twentieth-Century Literature* (1957); and Desmond E. S. Maxwell's "Edith Wharton and the Realists," *American Background* (1963). Percy Lubbock's "Henry James," *Letters* (1920), presents some pertinent criticism of Edith Wharton's art, as also does Louise Bogan's "Decoration of Novels," *Selected Criticism* (1955). There is a varied selection of critical remarks concerning Mrs. Wharton's technique in Dorothy Nyren's *A Library of Literary Criticism: Modern American Literature* (1964). Irving Howe, as editor, presents varied aspects of Mrs. Wharton's artistic capabilities, as well as analyses of individual works, in *Edith Wharton: A Collection of Critical Essays* (1962). Mrs. Wharton herself has stated some of her views on writing in several critical articles: "The Criticism of Fiction," *The Living Age* (1914); "Character and Situation in the Novel," *Scribner's* (1925); "Visibility in Fiction," *Yale Review;* and "Tendencies in Modern Fiction,"

Saturday Review of Literature (1934). Four doctoral dissertations, written since Mrs. Wharton's death, discuss her literary techniques: Walter B. Greenwood's "Edith Wharton: Her Materials and Methods," *University of Cincinnati* (1941); Nancy R. Leach's "Edith Wharton: Critic of American Life and Literature," University of Pennsylvania (1952); Millicent L. Bell's "Studies in a Writer's Development," Brown University (1955); and Melvin W. Askew's "Edith Wharton's Literary Theory," University of Oklahoma (1957). Lawson M. Melish's "Bibliography of the Collected Writings of Edith Wharton" was published in 1927. In 1933, two other bibliographies appeared: Edward K. Brown's "A Bibliography of the Writings of Edith Wharton," *American Literature* (November, 1933); and Lavinia R. Davis' "A Bibliography of the Writings of Edith Wharton," *Publisher's Weekly* (June 17, 1933).

CRITICISM WITH SPECIAL REFERENCE TO *ETHAN FROME*. Concerning specific criticism with regard to *Ethan Frome*, there has been much published. The following reviews and critical essays (both brief and extended) are listed and discussed in chronological order. In the year of its publication, 1911, *Ethan Frome* was reviewed by three American periodicals, the article in *The Nation* (October 26) being a good sampling. Mrs. Wharton's approach to her "chronicle" is seen as "assured and entirely individual," as well as "direct and firm." She is praised for her handling of the "theme of triumphant malice and tortured love." Also, the reviewer notes that she has captured the "melancholy spirit" typical of rural New England. Zenobia Frome is seen as a symbol of "fate." Praise in this review is echoed in two other critical articles published in America (*Scribner's*, August, 1911, and *Current Literature*, January 12, 1912). A London publication (*Bookman,* January, 1912) includes an essentially affirmative review of the short novel. In Mrs. Wharton's autobiography (*A Backward Glance,* 1934), she makes reference to the fact that some readers considered her tragic tale of New England as "painful"; she also writes that early reviewers "severely criticized" what was considered the "clumsy structure" of this work. (Note the follow-up discussion of this point in the commentary concerning

Mrs. Wharton's own "Introduction" to *Ethan Frome,* 1939.)
Percy Lubbock writes sensitively of *Ethan Frome* in "The
Novels of Edith Wharton," *Quarterly Review* (1915). He
emphasizes Mrs. Wharton's ability to effectively relate her
tale by using "small homely events," such as Ethan and
Mattie tramping home together through the snow, or the
breaking of the pickle dish. Elizabeth S. Sergeant's "Idealized New England: Mrs. Wharton's *Ethan Frome," New Republic* (1915), is a very exciting and stimulating comment
on the novel. This critic writes that *Ethan Frome* is not "life"—
but it is a "literary copy of it." Ethan is not seen as realistically
conceived, because he and Mattie would not have stopped
"for that preposterous coast to death." Something which they
could not possibly go against in their own natures would have
caused them to drive to the railroad station and to part
forever. The reviewer is very willing to praise Mrs. Wharton
for what she has accomplished by "creative imagination" and
for the "sharp yet delicate shadings" in the presentation of
the story. (Comparable in tone to the Sergeant criticism is a
later article by John Crowe Ransom, "Mrs. Wharton's Diffi-
culty," *American Review,* 1936.) Much later, in 1951, Blake
Nevius writes very affirmatively of *Ethan Frome* in *New
England Quarterly,* in respect to the main themes of Mrs.
Wharton's fiction revealed in this New England classic. Also,
Mr. Nevius's article, "Edith Wharton Today," in the *Pacific
Spectator* (1951), should be noted here. The same approximate point of view is established in 1928, when Osbert
Burdett, in an article entitled "Contemporary American Authors," (*London Mercury*) writes: *Ethan Frome* is "too like
a study of peasant life from a scholar's window to be a living
structure of the countryside." Edith Wharton's article, "The
Writing of *Ethan Frome," Colophon,* II (1931), proves to be
worthwhile. Ludwig Lewisohn's comment on *Ethan Frome,*
in *Expression in America* (1932), is comparable to the previous *London Mercury* criticism: Mrs. Wharton's "art . . .
is an art without spiritual vitality," for this particular fiction is
"a hothouse, not a garden." Granville Hicks, in *The Great
Tradition: An Interpretation of American Literature Since
the Civil War* (1935), writes of *Ethan Frome* as being "dram-
atically effective," but "somehow cold and mechanical." Ver-

non Loggins, in "Manners: Edith Wharton," *I Hear America. . . : Literature in the United States Since* 1900 (1937), feels that Mrs. Wharton's picture of people in western Massachusetts is "psychologically true." Mr. Loggins compares *Ethan Frome* to a Sophoclean drama and states that its prose has the emotional impact of fine poetry. He declares the work to be her "highest achievement as an artist." Bernard De Voto's "Introduction" to *Ethan Frome* (1938) is valuable reading. A readily available criticism is an "Introduction" Mrs. Wharton herself wrote for *Ethan Frome,* published in the 1939 Scribner Library edition of the work. The article is brief—but to the point. In the first place, she states how she happened to write *Ethan Frome*: to picture life as it actually was in the small hill villages in New England. (Originally, it was begun as an exercise in writing in French, when Mrs. Wharton wanted to improve her skill in French.) In the second place, she justifies why she chose the particular literary framework which she used: to tell the story from several points of view, with flashbacks and an anti-climax which follows the main part of the "tragedy" by a generation. J. A. Randall's *"Ethan Frome," Publisher's Weekly* (1940) includes some pertinent facts about the work. Van Wyck Brooks, in *New England Indian Summer*: 1865-1915 (1940), refers to the plot of *Ethan Frome* as "fictitious"—that is, created by art as opposed to nature; he also suggests that the reader has the feeling that a "superior person" is looking over the "squalid affairs of these children of fate" (Ethan, Mattie, and Zeena). Alfred Kazin's 1942 comment on *Ethan Frome* is quite direct and provocative: he writes of the novel as "not a New England story," and he points out that Mrs. Wharton "knew little of the New England common world." This same point is pursued by Gordon Hall Gerould, in "The Modern World in the Novel," *The Patterns of English and American Fiction: A History* (1942), when he writes that Mrs. Wharton "knew the life of New England only as a summer resident." George Snell, in "Edith Wharton and Willa Cather," *The Shapers of American Fiction*: 1798-1947 (1947), writes of *Ethan Frome* as Mrs. Wharton's "best work"—but he adds that one is left with the "impression" that it is a "manufactured" creation, the work of an "accomplished craftsman." Mr. Snell goes on to state that

Ethan as a character is less well realized than Zeena, that Mattie is the "fulcrum for the tragedy" (balancing point), and that the "situation is melodramatic." Edward Wagenknecht in "Edith Wharton: Social Background and Ethical Dilemma," *Cavalcade of the American Novel* (1952), refers to *Ethan Frome* as a "cool, spare tragedy," and he briefly discusses Mrs. Wharton's storytelling "device." Blake Nevius's 1953 essay, "On *Ethan Frome*," in Irving Howe's *Edith Wharton: A Collection of Critical Essays* (1962), discusses in detail the characters pictured and techniques illustrated in the novel. J. D. Thomas' "Marginalia on *Ethan Frome*," *American Literature* (1955), is of interest. The thought processes and observations of the male storyteller are seen as not typical of a man, the time pattern of the novel seems to be incorrectly conceived, and Ethan's moral crisis (when he finally decides against asking the Hales for financial assistance) appears to be motivated by confusing impulses on his part. Lionel Trilling has a fascinating essay, "The Morality of Inertia," in Robert MacIver, ed., *Great Moral Dilemmas* (1956), which indicates that *Ethan Frome* "presents no moral issue." (The explanation of this view in connection with Aristotle is very interesting.) Nancy R. Leach's interesting essay, "New England in the Stories of Edith Wharton," *New England Quarterly* (1957), is stimulating reading for fans of Mrs. Wharton's works. In the third and longest of three unfinished Wharton manuscripts, *New England*, there are several "resemblances" to Ethan Frome. The setting is "similar," and the three major characters are reminiscent of those in the 1911 novel. Lucius Torrey, a farmer, has "frustrated intellectual ambitions" and an "unfortunate marriage." His wife, Thyrze, has "imaginary ailments." Alida Gage enters the picture, and one may imagine a future relationship developing between Lucius and Alida, comparable to that between Ethan Frome and Mattie Silver. Ina Honaker Herron's "The Town, the Brahmins, and Others," *The Small Town in American Literature* (1959), includes a glowing reference to *Ethan Frome*, describing it as a "masterpiece," for the superior presentation of "aspect, dialect, and mental and moral attitudes" of the characters. In 1960, Willard Thorp (*American Writing in the Twentieth Century*) writes that *Ethan Frome* is one of Mrs. Wharton's four or five novels which will find a "permanent place" in our literature. This critic sees the narrator as "needless" and "rather too fastidious." Millicent Bell's *Edith Wharton and Henry James: The Story of Their Friendship* (1965) reveals some of the sources for *Ethan Frome*. Dr. Gene Barnett, in an unpublished note, offers the suggestion that the name "Starkfield" is a combination of the names of two towns, almost equidistant from Lenox, Massachusetts—probably the locale for *Ethan Frome*. The two towns are *Stock*bridge and Pitts*field*. (The nineteenth century pronunciation for "*Stock*" might well be slurred to sound like "*Stark*.")

Literary students of Mrs. Wharton's works are looking forward with eager anticipation to 1968 when there will be open for inspection a collection of her manuscripts and papers, including letters. This collection is in the Yale Collection of American Literature in the Yale University Library. After the student has finished reading *Ethan Frome*, he would do well to review the structure and point of view of the novel in the light of the following two references: Edith Wharton's "Constructing a Novel," *The Writing of Fiction* (1925); and Norman Friedman's "Point of View in Fiction: The Development of a Critical Concept," *Publications of the Modern Language Association* (1955). Interest in *Ethan Frome* is still at a high peak. Louis Auchincloss, as editor of *The Edith Wharton Reader* (1965), includes this classic of New England farm life in its entirety, among briefer selections of fiction. Discussions still rage over whether *Ethan Frome* is a realistic picture of Massachusetts farm life or a highly artificial, literary creation. There are defenders for each view. Perhaps the best procedure is for each reader to decide for himself the degree of realism it represents to him.

DRAMATIZATION OF ETHAN FROME

A few words should be added about the very successful stage presentation of this classic: Owen Davis and Donald Davis' *Ethan Frome* (*A Dramatization of Edith Wharton's Novel*) (1936). The play, which is dedicated to Edith Wharton, has a "Foreword" by Mrs. Wharton herself, who heartily approves the dramatic version of this work. There are five divisions: a prologue, three acts, and an epilogue. The setting is divided among the following places: the outside and inside of the Frome farmhouse; outside the Starkfield Congregational Church; and the top of the hill near Starkfield. The dialogue is much more filled with dialectal expressions than Mrs. Wharton's original work. There is constant use of the word "A-yeah"—a country expression indicating agreement of the fact that one is listening to what someone else is saying. Ethan's speeches are generally very brief—entirely in keeping with the concept of Ethan as a man of few words. One interesting change between the novel and the dramatization is as follows: in the novel, Ethan himself realizes that he cannot ask Andrew Hale for money by taking advantage of him with a false request for financial aid to hire a servant for Zeena; in the play, Zeena tells Ethan that he cannot take advantage of Mr. Hale, because of the builder's kindness. In the dramatization, the crash of the sled into the elm is not seen. The scene ends, as from off-stage can be heard the sound of the sled runners gathering speed in the race down the icy hill.

SUBJECT BIBLIOGRAPHY AND GUIDE TO
RESEARCH PAPERS

The research paper should be based upon careful reading of the text of *Ethan Frome,* which is found in numerous editions. An excellent paperback is the Scribner Library edition, published by Charles Scribner's Sons. This edition includes Mrs. Wharton's own "Introduction" to *Ethan Frome.*

A considerable amount of criticism has been written about Mrs. Wharton and her works. The following selective items include the most important critical commentaries about her life, her career as an artist, *Ethan Frome,* and several of her other outstanding works of fiction. The bibliographical listings are made alphabetically by author for each research topic.

(1) GENERAL: STANDARD CRITICISM AND INTERPRETATION

Questions to consider: How has critical opinion concerning Mrs. Wharton's work changed since 1900? What are the main themes (or ideas) explored in her works? Is her work distinctive and individual enough to set her off from other writers of her period? What is the general consensus of opinion today concerning her place in American literature?

Auchincloss, Louis, *Edith Wharton* (University of Minnesota pamphlets on American Writers) (1961).

————, ed., *The Edith Wharton Reader* (1965).

Beach, Joseph Warren, *Twentieth-Century Novel: Studies in Technique* (1932).

Bell, Millicent, *Edith Wharton and Henry James: The Story of Their Friendship* (1965).

Boynton, Percy H., "Edith Wharton," *English Journal* (1923).

Brooks, Van Wyck, *New England Indian Summer: 1865-1915* (1940).

————, *The Confident Years: 1885-1915* (1952).

Brown, Edward K., "Edith Wharton," *Etudes Anglaises* (1938).

————, *Edith Wharton: Etude Critique* (1935).

Coolidge, Bertha, "Mrs. Wharton's Works," *Saturday Review of Literature* (1933).

Davis, Lavinia R., "A Bibliography of the Writings of Edith Wharton," (1933).

Davis, Owen, and Donald Davis, *Ethan Frome* (*A Dramatization of Edith Wharton's Novel* (1936).

Dwight, H. G., "The Work of Mrs. Wharton," *Putnam's* (1908).

Fremantle, Anne, "Edith Wharton: Values and Vulgarity," in Harold C. Gardiner, S. J., ed., *Fifty Years of the American Novel: A Christian Appraisal* (1952).

Gerould, K. F., *Edith Wharton: A Critical Study* (1922).

Green, Paul, and Elizabeth L. Green, *Contemporary American Literature: A Study of Fourteen Outstanding American Writers* (1925).

Hartwick, Harry, *The Foreground of American Fiction* (1934).

Harvey, John, "Contrasting Worlds," A Study in the Novels of Edith Wharton," *Etudes Anglaises* (1954).

Hoffman, Frederick, *The Modern Novel in America: 1900-1950* (1951).

Howe, Irving, ed., *Edith Wharton : A Collection of Critical Essays* (1962).

————, "The Achievement of Edith Wharton," In Irving

Howe, ed., *Edith Wharton: A Collection of Critical Essays* (1962).

Kunitz, Stanley J., ed., *Living Authors* (1931).

Lovett, Robert, *Edith Wharton* (1925).

Lubbock, Percy, *A Portrait of Edith Wharton* (1947).

Macy, J. A., *The Spirit of American Literature* (1912).

Melish, Lawson M., *A Bibliography of the Collected Writings of Edith Wharton* (1927).

Millett, Fred B., *Contemporary American Authors* (1940).

Morley, Christopher D., *Streamlines* (1936).

Nevius, Blake, *Edith Wharton: A Study of Her Fiction* (1953).

Quinn, Arthur Hobson, *American Fiction: An Historical and Critical Survey* (1936).

Sedgwick, Henry D., "The Novels of Mrs. Wharton," *Atlantic Monthly* (1906).

Sholl, Anna M., "The Works of Edith Wharton," *Gunton's* (1903).

Snell, George, *The Shapers of American Fiction* (1947).

Squire, Sir John C., and others, *Contemporary American Authors* (1928).

Taylor, Walter F., *A History of American Letters* (1936).

Van Doren, Carl, *Contemporary American Novelists* (1922).

Ward, Alfred C., *American Literature, 1880-1930* (1932).

Wharton, Edith, *A Backward Glance* (1934).

Wharton, Edith, *Book Review Digest* (1906-13, 1915-21, 1923-30, 1932-34, 1936-38).

Wharton, Edith, *The Writing of Fiction* (1925).

(2) EDITH WHARTON'S LIFE

Questions to consider: What was her family background? Where did she live and travel? How did Europe influence her literary work? Who and what were some of the major influences on her thought?

Brooks, Van Wyck, "Edith Wharton," *The Confident Years: 1885-1915* (1952).

Burdett, Osbert, "Edith Wharton," in J. C. Squire, ed., *Contemporary American Authors* (1928).

Canby, Henry E., "Edith Wharton," *Saturday Review of Literature* (1937).

Carroll, E., "Visit with Edith Wharton," *Delineator* (1932).

Chandler, W., "Winters in Paris," *Atlantic Monthly* (1936).

Gray, James, "Very Important Personages," *On Second Thought* (1946).

Halsey, Francis W., *Women Authors of Our Day in Their Homes* (1903).

Herrick, R., "Mrs. Wharton's World," *New Republic* (1915).

Kunitz, Stanley J., ed., *Living Authors* (1931).

Loggins, Vernon, "Manners: Edith Wharton," *I Hear America . . . : Literature in the United States Since 1900* (1937).

Lubbock Percy, *A Portrait of Edith Wharton* (1947).

"Portrait," *Saturday Review of Literature* (1944).

Morgan, H. Wayne, "Edith Wharton: The Novelist of Manners and Morals," *Writers in Transition: Seven Americans* (1963).

Overton, Grant, *Authors of the Day* (1924).

"Portrait," *Ladies' Home Journal* (1930).

"Portrait" *Bookman* (1932).

"Portrait," *Literary Digest* (1922, 1923).

"Portrait," *Literary Review* (1924).

"Portrait," *Mentor* (1929).

"Portrait," *Mentor* (1927).

"Portrait," *Publisher's Weekly* (1950).

"Portrait," *Saturday Review* (1952).

"Portrait," *Woman's Home Companion* (1919).

"Portrait," *Woman's Journal* (1929).

Repplier, Agnes, "Edith Wharton," *Commonwealth* (1938).

Sencourt, Robert, "Edith Wharton," *Cornhill Magazine* (1938).

————, "The Poetry of Edith Wharton," *Bookman* (1931).

Swan, Michael, "The Early Edith Wharton," *A Small Part of Time* (1961).

Wharton, Edith, "A Backward Glance," *Ladies' Home Journal* (1933).

Wharton, Edith, "Obituary," *Commonwealth, Newsweek, Publisher's Weekly,* and *Time* (1937).

Willcox, Louise C., "Edith Wharton," *Outlook* (1905).

Wilson, E., "Review of P. Lubbock's *Portrait of Edith Wharton*," *New Yorker* (1947).

(3) EDITH WHARTON AS A WOMAN NOVELIST

Questions to consider: Does she reflect only the woman's point of view in her fiction? What about the criticism suggesting that she approaches her literary works with the logic of a man? Is this a justified criticism?

Auchincloss, Louis, *Pioneers and Caretakers: A Study of Nine American Women Novelists* (1965).

Collins, Joseph, "Big Four of American Women Writers," *Taking the Literary Pulse: Psychological Studies of Life and Letters* (1924).

Coxe, L. O., "What Edith Wharton Saw in Innocence," *New Republic* (1955).

Gilbertson, Catherine, "Mrs. Wharton, an Agate Lamp Within Thy Hand," (1929).

Jessup, Josephine Lurie, *The Faith of Our Feminists: A Study of the Novels of Edith Wharton, Ellen Glasgow, Willa Cather* (1950).

Kazin, A., "Lady and the Tiger," *Virginia Quarterly Review* (1941).

Lawrence, M., "Helpmeets," *School of Femininity* (1936).

Lawrence, Margaret, *We Write as Women* (1937).

Leach, Nancy R., "Edith Wharton's Unpublished Novel," *American Literature* (1953).

Mansfield, Katherine, *Novels and Novelists* (1930).

Overton, Grant, *The Women Who Make Our Novels* (1928).

Pattee, Fred Lewis, "The Feminine Novel," *The New American Literature* (1930).

Roberts, Richard E., "Edith Wharton," *Bookman* (1923).

(4) MRS. WHARTON: A MASTER OF LITERARY TECHNIQUE

Questions to consider: What is individual about her literary style? What are the outstanding characteristics of her writing technique? What is her basic philosophy concerning her composition of prose? Does she experiment with a variety of techniques? Is she interested in naturalism as a form of writing? Is her fiction art or propaganda?

Ames, Van Meter, "The Technique of the Novel," *Aesthetics of the Novel* (1928).

Askew, Melvin W., "Edith Wharton's Literary Theory," Ph.D. dissertation, University of Oklahoma (1957).

Beach, Joseph Warren, *The Twentieth-Century Novel: Studies in Technique* (1932).

Bell, Millicent L., "Edith Wharton: Studies in a Writer's Development," Ph.D. dissertation, Brown University (1955).

Bjorkman, Edwin A., "The Greater Edith Wharton," *Voices of Tomorrow* (1913).

Boynton, H. W., "Mrs. Wharton's Manner," *Nation* (1913).

Boynton, Percy H., *Some Contemporary Americans* (1924).

Brown, E. K., "Mrs. Wharton," in Pelham Edgar's *The Art of the Novel from 1700 to the Present Time* (1933).

Collins, Joseph, *Taking the Literary Pulse* (1924).

Cooper, F. T., "Critical Study of Mrs. Wharton," *Some American Story Tellers* (1911).

Cross, Wilbur L., "Edith Wharton," *Bookman* (1926).

"Edith Wharton: Two Conflicting Estimates of Her Art," *Current Opinion* (1915).

Follett, Helen Thomas, and Wilson Follett, "Edith Wharton," *Some Modern Novelists: Appreciations and Estimates* (1919).

Friedman, Norman, "Point of View in Fiction: The Development of a Critical Concept," *Publications of the Modern Language Association* (1955).

Gerould, Gordon Hall, "The Modern World in the Novel," *The Patterns of English and American Fiction: A History* (1942).

Greenwood, Walter B., "Edith Wharton: Her Materials and Methods," Ph.D. dissertation, University of Cincinnati (1941).

Hackett, F., "Mrs. Wharton's Art," *New Republic* (1917).

Hatcher, Harlan H., "Realism and the Public Taste: 1900-1921," *Creating the Modern American Novel* (1935).

Hoffman, Freedrick J., "Point of Moral Reference: A Compromise Study of Edith Wharton and F. Scott Fitzgerald," in *English Institute Essays* (1949).

James, Henry, *Notes on Novelists* (1914).

Kazin, Alfred, "Two Educations: Edith Wharton and Theodore Dreiser," *On Native Grounds* (1942).

Lovett, Robert M., *Edith Wharton* (1925).

Lubbock, Percy, "The Novels of Edith Wharton," *Quarterly Review* (1915).

Lynskey, Winifred, "The 'Heroes' of Edith Wharton," *University of Toronto Quarterly* (1954).

Marble, Annie R., *A Study of the Modern Novel, British and American Since 1900* (1928).

Maxwell, Desmond E. S., "Edith Wharton and The Realists," *American Fiction: The Intellectual Background* (1963).

McCole, C. J., "Some Notes on Edith Wharton," *Catholic World,* (1938).

Michaud, Regis, *The American Novel To-day, A Social and Psychological Study* (1928).

Nevius, Blake, *Edith Wharton: A Study of Her Fiction* (1953).

Nyren, Dorothy, *A Library of Literary Criticism: Modern American Literature* (1964).

O'Connor, William Van, "The Novel of Experience," *Critique* (1956).

Overton, Grant, *American Nights Entertainment* (1923).

Overton, Grant, *An Hour of the American Novel* (1929).

Pattee, Fred Lewis, *The New American Literature* (1930).

Phelps, William L., "Appreciation," *Delineator* (1932).

Ransom, John Crowe, "Characters and Character," *American Review* (1936).

Rubin, Larry, "Aspects of Naturalism in Four Novels by Edith Wharton," *Twentieth-Century Literature* (1957).

Russell, Frances, "Edith Wharton's Use of Imagery," *English Journal* (1932).

Sedgwick, Henry D., "The Art of Mrs. Wharton," *The New American Type and Other Essays* (1908).

Sherman, Stuart P., "Edith Wharton: Costuming the Passions," *The Main Stream* (1927).

Snell, George, "Edith Wharton and Willa Cather," *The Shapers of American Fiction: 1798-1947* (1947).

Stewart, J. T., "Appreciations," *Saturday Review of Literature* (1937).

Straumann, Heinrich, *American Literature in the Twentieth Century* (1951).

"These are Sturdy Tales," *Newsweek* (1958).

Trueblood, Charles K., "Edith Wharton," *Dial* (1920).

Tuttleton, James W., "Edith Wharton and the Novel of Manners," Ph.D. dissertation, University of North Carolina.

Underwood, John C., "Culture and Edith Wharton," *Literature and Insurgency* (1914).

Van Doren, Carl, "Tradition and Transition," *The American Novel: 1789-1939* (1940).

Wagenknecht, Edward C., "Affirmation: Of Art and of Life," *Cavalcade of the American Novel* (1952).

Wharton, Edith, "Character and Situation in the Novel," *Scribner's Magazine* (1925).

Wharton, Edith, "Confessions of a Novelist," *The Atlantic Monthly* (1933).

Wharton, Edith, "Great American Novel," *Yale Review* (1927).

Wharton, Edith, "Tendencies in Modern Fiction," *Saturday Review of Literature* (1934).

Wharton, Edith, "The Criticism of Fiction," *The Living Age* (1914).

Wharton, Edith, "The Writing of *Ethan Frome*," *Colophon*, II (1931).

Wharton, Edith, *The Writing of Fiction* (1925).

Wharton, Edith, "Visibility in Fiction," *Yale Review* (1929).

Williams, Blanche C., "Edith Wharton," *Our Short Story Writers* (1920).

Winters, Calvin, "Edith Wharton," *American Bookman* (1911).

(5) INFLUENCES UPON MRS. WHARTON'S THOUGHT AND LITERARY TECHNIQUE

Questions to consider: What writers did she admire? Which ones did she read for models of her own work? Which of her friends most influenced her thought and style?

Fife, Hilda, "Letters from Edith Wharton to Vernon Lee," *Colby Library Quarterly* (1953).

Flanner, Janet, "Dearest Edith," *The New Yorker* (1929).

Hind, Charles, "Edith Wharton," *Authors and I* (1921).

James, Henry, *Notes on Novelists* (1914).

Leavis, Q. D., "Henry James's Heiress: The Importance of Edith Wharton," *Scrutiny* (1938).

Lubbock, Percy, "Henry James," *Letters*, Vol. I (1920).

Wharton, Edith, "George Eliot," *Bookman* (1902).

Wharton, Edith, "Reconsideration of Proust," *Saturday Review of Literature* (1934).

Wharton, Edith, "William C. Brownell," *Scribner's Magazine* (1928).

Wharton, Edith, "Marcel Proust," *Yale Review* (1925).

(6) MRS. WHARTON'S PHILOSOPHY AND SOCIAL CRITICISM

Questions to consider: Did Mrs. Wharton have any particular philosophy of life which differed from that of her contemporaries or her social equals? What were some of her basic philosophical beliefs? Did she use her philosophical point of view as a point of departure when she satirized social situations and institutions?

Follett, Helen Thomas, and Wilson Follett, "Edith Wharton," *Some Modern Novelists: Appreciations and Estimates* (1919).

Herron, Ina Honaker, "The Town, the Brahmins, and Others," *The Small Town in American Literature* (1959).

Howe, Irving, "A Reading of *The House of Mirth*," from "Introduction," by Irving Howe to Edith Wharton's *The House of Mirth* (1962).

Leach, Nancy R., "Edith Wharton: Critic of American Life and Literature," Ph.D. dissertation, University of Pennsylvania (1952).

Lyde, M. J., *Edith Wharton: Convention and Morality in the Work of a Novelist* (1959).

————, "The Theory and Treatment of Morality in the Work of Edith Wharton," Ph.D. dissertation, University of Chicago (1956).

McCall, Raymond G., "Attitudes toward Wealth in the Fiction of Edith Wharton, Theodore Dreiser, and F. Scott Fitzgerald," Ph.D. dissertation, University of Wisconsin.

Michaud, Regis, *The American Novel To-day, a Social and Psychological Study* (1928).

Monroe, N. E., "Moral Situation in Edith Wharton," *Novel and Society* (1940).

Nevius, Blake, *Edith Wharton* (1953).

Parrington, Vernon Louis, *Main Currents in American Thought*, Vol. III (1930).

Parrington, Vernon L., "Our Literary Aristocrat," *The Pacific Review* (1921).

Rice, Mary Lund, "The Moral Conservatism of Edith Wharton," Ph.D. dissertation, University of Minnesota (1953).

Rideout, Walter B., "Edith Wharton's *The House of Mirth*," in Charles Shapiro, ed., *Twelve Original Essays on Great American Novels* (1958).

Saunders, Thomas, "Moral Values in the Novels of Edith Wharton," Ph.D. dissertation, University of Pittsburgh (1954).

Wagenknecht, Edward C., "Edith Wharton: Social Background and Ethical Dilemma," *Cavalcade of the American Novel* (1952).

Waldstein, Charles, "Social Ideals," *North American Review* (1906).

Wharton, Edith, "Permanent Values in Fiction," *Saturday Review of Literature* (1934).

(7) MRS. WHARTON AND THE WORLD OF ART

Questions to consider: Did Mrs. Wharton call on her own knowledge and appreciation of art and architecture when she pictured her settings in her works? What is the role played by the amateur or the professional artist in her writing? Does she seem sincere in her admiration of art?

Basinger, Mary, "Edith Wharton and the Fine Arts," Ph.D. dissertation, Ohio State University.

Bogan, Louise, "Decoration of Novels," *Selected Criticism* (1955).

Fritz, Alphonse J., "The Use of the Arts of Decoration in Edith Wharton's Fiction: A Study of Her Interests in Architecture, Interior Decoration, and Gardening," Ph.D. dissertation, University of Wisconsin (1956).

Wharton, Edith, *Italian Villas* (1904).

Wharton, Edith, and Ogden Codman, *The Decoration of Houses* (1897).

(8) CRITICAL OPINION ABOUT MRS. WHARTON AND HER WORK SINCE HER DEATH IN 1937

Questions to consider: Since Mrs. Wharton's death in 1937, how does representative criticism vary in its appraisal of her art and literary contribution? Do some critics severely condemn her works and others highly praise them? Is there a tendency in the later criticism to minimize the influence of

Henry James? Do most of the critics generally agree with each other about her place in American letters?

"Age of Edith," *Newsweek* (1962).

Bogan, Louise, *Selected Criticism* (1955).

"Last Survivor," *Time* (1964).

Monroe, Nellie Elizabeth, *The Novel and Society* (1941).

Nyren, D., ed., "Edith Wharton," A *Library of Literary Criticism* (1964).

Straumann, Heinrich, *American Literature in The Twentieth Century* (1951).

Thorp, Willard, *American Writing in the Twentieth Century* (1960).

Trilling, Diana, "*The House of Mirth* Revisited," in Irving Howe, ed., *Edith Wharton: A Collection of Critical Essays* (1962).

Wagenknecht, Edward C., *Cavalcade of the American Novel* (1952).

Wilson, Edmund, "A Memoir of Edith Wharton," *Classics and Commercials* (1950).

————, Edmund, "Justice to Edith Wharton," *The New Republic* (1938). Also, in Wilson, Edmund, *The Wound and the Bow.*

(9) MRS. WHARTON'S SOCIAL CRITICISM

Questions to consider: Is Mrs. Wharton's criticism of social life reserved only for the *nouveau riche* (new money) group? Or, is it aimed, to some extent, at the older, conservative members of society? Is there conflict between two social groups in most of Mrs. Wharton's fiction—even in *Ethan Frome?* Is there always a struggle between the conventional, conservative members of the community and a new rebelling group? Is Mrs. Wharton without pity for the objects of her critical satire? Does she have a sense of humor?

Auchincloss, Louis, "Edith Wharton and Her New Yorks," *Reflections of a Jacobite* (1961).

Boas, Ralph P., and Katherine Burton, *Social Backgrounds of American Literature* (1933).

Brooks, Van Wyck, and Otto L. Bettmann, "New York High Society," *Our Literary Heritage* (1956).

Gelfant, Blanche H., "Sherwood Anderson, Edith Wharton, and Thomas Wolfe," *The American City Novel* (1954).

Horton, Rod W., "Social and Individual Values in the New York Stories of Edith Wharton," Ph.D. dissertation, New York University (1945).

"Little Girl's New York," *Harper's Magazine* (1938).

Morris, Lloyd R., "Lady Vanishes," *Postscript to Yesterday; America: the Last Fifty Years* (1947).

Overton, Grant, "Edith Wharton's Old New York," *Cargoes for Crusoes* (1924).

Sherman, S. P., "Edith Wharton: Costuming the Passions," *Main Stream* (1927).

(10) *ETHAN FROME* AS A WORK OF REALISM

Questions to consider: Is *Ethan Frome* the realistic picture of New England country life which some critics declare it to be? Is there any justification for the idea that *Ethan Frome* comes close to being a perfectly constructed work of art? Is it actually an artificial "hothouse" creation? For example, *would* Ethan and Mattie have taken their near-fatal ride down the hill? Or instead, would they have dumbly and pathetically parted forever at the railroad station?

Brooks, Van Wyck, *New England Indian Summer: 1865-1915* (1940).

Burdett, Osbert, "Contemporary American Authors," *London Mercury* (1928).

De Voto, Bernard, "Introduction to *Ethan Frome*" (1938).

Ethan Frome reviews: *Bookman* (London) (1912); *Scribner's* (1911); *Nation* (1911); *Current Literature* (1912).

Herron, Ina Honaker, "The Town, the Brahmins, and Others," *The Small Town in American Literature* (1959).

Hicks, Granville, *The Great Tradition: An Interpretation of American Literature Since the Civil War* (1935).

Leach, Nancy R., "New England in the Stories of Edith Wharton," *New England Quarterly* (1957).

Lewissohn, Ludwig, *Expression in America* (1932).

Nevius, Blake, *Edith Wharton: A Study of Her Fiction* (1953).

Randall, D. A. (notes by J. T. Winterich), "Ethan Frome," *Publisher's Weekly* (1940).

Ransom, J. C., "Characters and Character," *American Review* (1936).

"Review of *Ethan Frome*," *The Nation* (1911).

Russell, Frances T., "Melodramatic Mrs. Wharton," *Sewanee Review* (1932).

Sergeant, Elizabeth S., "Idealized New England; Mrs. Wharton's *Ethan Frome*," *New Republic* (1915).

Snell, George, "Edith Wharton and Willa Cather," *The Shapers of American Fiction: 1798-1947* (1947).

Thomas, J. D., "Marginalia on *Ethan Frome*," *American Literature* (1955).

Trilling, Lionel, "The Morality of Inertia," in Robert MacIver, ed., *Great Moral Dilemmas* (1956).

Wharton, Edith, "Introduction," *Ethan Frome* (1939).

ADDITIONAL TOPICS FOR FURTHER RESEARCH ON *ETHAN FROME*

1. Characters surrounded by forces beyond their own powers to control.
2. Poverty and the code of the village as they dominate the characters.
3. The bareness of the dialogue.
4. The role played by the numerous meals eaten.
5. Frustrated women.
6. Determinism (heredity and environment) as it affects the characters.
7. Elements of naturalism.
8. Reflection of nineteenth century Puritanism.
9. Moral decisions facing characters.
10. Setting as a character.
11. Women who are cruel and soulless.
12. Natural settings viewed as artificially landscaped gardens.
13. Use of British vocabulary.
14. Characters upset by small incidents and details.
15. Use of irony.
16. Women characters stronger than men characters.
17. Rebellious characters.
18. Selfishness in all the characters.
19. Introspection in Ethan.
20. Reflection of the atmosphere of the novel through furnishings.

NOTES

NOTES

NOTES

NOTES

NOTES

NOTES

NOTES

NOTES

NOTES

NOTES

<u>VOCAB</u>

ominous - threatening

innocuous - harmless

opulence - wealth

curtly - in a few words; lotharge

tenuous - very thin

taunt - scornfull remark

NOTES

MONARCH® NOTES AND STUDY GUIDES

ARE AVAILABLE AT RETAIL STORES EVERYWHERE

In the event your local bookseller cannot provide you with other Monarch titles you want—

ORDER ON THE FORM BELOW:

Simply send retail price, local sales tax, if any, plus 25¢ to cover mailing & handling.

Complete order form appears on inside front & back covers for your convenience.

IBM #	AUTHOR & TITLE (exactly as shown on title listing)	PRICE
	PLUS ADD'L FOR POSTAGE	25¢
	GRAND TOTAL	

MONARCH® PRESS, a division of Simon & Schuster, Inc.
Mail Service Department, 1 West 39th Street, New York, N.Y. 10018

I enclose............................dollars to cover retail price, local sales tax, plus mailing and handling.

Name_____
(Please print)

Address_____

City_____ State_____ Zip_____

Please send check or money order. We cannot be responsible for cash.